A HISTORY OF
Medieval Latin Literature

A HISTORY OF
Medieval Latin Literature

By

MAURICE HÉLIN

REVISED EDITION

Translated by

JEAN CHAPMAN SNOW

New York · WILLIAM SALLOCH · *1949*

This book is translated from

Littérature d'Occident:
Histoire des Lettres Latines du Moyen Age

Printed in U. S. A.
THE WILLIAM BYRD PRESS, INC., RICHMOND, VA.

Contents

A HISTORY OF
Medieval Latin Literature

Introduction

To PUT in 120 pages the history of a millennium of an extremely rich literature would seem to be a wager. If we have hazarded an attempt, it is because the subject, in spite of a century of erudite research (which has considerably increased during the last thirty years) is still unknown. There is surely no one at present who is ignorant of the importance of an epoch in which modern civilization arose, and everyone knows that Latin (which at the time assured the spiritual unity of Western Europe) was the language of theological treatises, philosophical summas, annals and chronicles, encyclopedias and edifying manuals.

The volumes of the *Patrologia* by Migne, or the folios of the *Monumenta* which contain so many of those works, are certainly not of an inviting appearance. Only a specialist would venture into them. Yet, the *Imitation of Christ* is still read (certainly more than any philosophical treatise of Cicero or Seneca) and the Christian folk still hear and sing the *Dies Irae* or the *Pange Lingua* every day. As incomplete or as imperfect as it might be, a short book on the history of these texts which still inspire and which are such strangers to us can be useful.

Among the multitude of works which we will treat (whose mass is infinitely greater than that of all the literature of antiquity) we shall deliberately leave aside all those which for us have become illegible: glosses, commentaries, compilations, a whole scholastic production whose importance we must not underestimate and which stamped medieval Latin literature with one of its most characteristic traits. We will also have to neglect (once past the pre-Carolingian period whose dearth of material makes everything important) any work of history, didacticism or edification which does not show the personality of the author. In short, we use the word literature in its narrowest sense, taking the risk of giving our readers an incomplete and, at times, inexact view of the field. We are resigned to it, for one does not see the most profound characteristics of a country at the first visit. As the tourist is first shown the great monuments and picturesque sites so shall we point out especially the works of imagination.

The dates 500 and 1500 sharply define the epoch within which we are going to follow the development of Latin literature. The simple reason of convenience seemed to suggest as a beginning the point where most of the works concerned with classic Latin literature stop. Even Labriolle's *History and Literature of Christianity* scarcely conducts us beyond the threshold of the Middle Ages. We would have preferred going back several centuries: whether it was to look in the poems of Commodian or in the alphabetical psalm of Saint Augustine for the germ of the tendencies which were not fully developed until the 11th century, or whether (as Maurice Wilmotte did in *Les Origines du Roman Français,* Paris, 1941) to find in the Apocryphal Gospels, the Acts of the Martyrs, and even in the treatises in which the Church Fathers denounced the scandalous morals of their time, the romanesque themes which were to nourish the imaginative literature of the centuries to come.

Such as they are, the dates 500 and 1500 (aside from the fact that every arbitrary division in the flow of time is misleading) have the advantage of not coinciding with those commonly assigned as the limits of the Middle Ages. This contributes to dissolve an equivocation: medieval Latin literature is not merely the continuation of Latin literature beyond antiquity. The distinction is a matter of nature, not of chronology. It is a new literature, Latin in expression, owing much to former centuries, yet born and living in its own surroundings.

The Genesis of Medieval Latin

It is ordinarily in a young people overflowing with vigor that one sees literature develop, at a time when their welfare and security are assured and their aristocracy seeks diversion. The literature with which we now concern ourselves was born in a ruined empire: a world in the process of dying. Barbarian hordes overran all the provinces at will. Carthage and the Eternal City, Rome, had been pillaged. We can sense a definitive disaster, and the gravest symptom from the standpoint of literature was that language itself had suffered an irreparable blow. It was not a question of style in a decadent literature: this overripeness which captured the imagination of Des Esseintes, "this particular flavor which Christianity was to add to a pagan language that was already ripe venison!"[1] The roots of the trouble are to be found elsewhere.[2] Certain unmistakable signs (since the age of the Republic) had pointed out an alteration of the Latin. The pronunciation especially was affected. The quantity of vowels went unnoticed, at least by the illiterate mass of the people.

[1] J. K. Huysmans, *A Rebours.*
[2] We recapitulate in broad outline the suggestive article by F. Lot, *A quelle époque a-t-on cessé de parler Latin?* (A.L.M.A. VI, 1931, pp. 97-159). On the other hand, Dag Norberg (Syntaktische Forschungen, Uppsala, 1943, pp. 11-25), comes to the conclusion that, however bastardized it appeared to be, the language remained faithful to its inner laws and continued to obey its proper nature until the moment when the Carolingian Renaissance established the reign of School-Latin and completed the break with the past.

The intensity of accent also replaced the sharpness of accent. From this came a new rhythm based on the succession of weak and strong vowels. In one stroke, classical poetry with its long and short feet and rhythmic prose with its metric clauses became unintelligible. At the same time, morphology and syntax changed. This process of disintegration, manifest in the third century, reached its fullest extent in the fifth century. We should not allow ourselves to be deceived by the literary output of the era. It is overfull of rhetoric (the fault lies with the schools) and it actually does not reflect the true state of the common language. "Latin letters from the third to the fifth century are the work of professionals, sometimes of great persons for whom a knowledge of fine classic (and therefore archaic) Latin is a mark of nobility and a high form of Roman patriotism" (F. Lot, *op. cit.* p. 114). "Truthfully," says Lot (p. 128), "the Latin texts of the fifth century and the first half of the sixth have only the appearance of life . . . one wrote a language which nobody spoke, even in the upper classes of society. Consequently, good usage no longer upheld the writing." After the invasions had closed the provincial schools and prevented the elite from communicating with the centers in which the traditions of good language were maintained—Rome, Milan, Ravenna—little time was needed for ignorance and barbarism to encroach upon even the most official writings: scrolls of the royal chancellery, laws and edicts of the kings. This was to be the predominant condition until the Carolingian Renaissance.

If they had been nothing more than representatives of ancient letters in the midst of the invading barbarians, a Boethius, a Cassiodorus, and later an Isidore of Seville, would have no claim here. They were, however, the embalmers of a dying culture and contributed, each in his own way, to passing the torch to future ages which could light new fires of civilization. For us, Boethius (c. 480-524) is above all the author of the *De Consolatione Philosophiae,* a work still revered but scarcely read. Perhaps our present troubled time will lead back to it readers better prepared to understand it. Boethius who belonged to the highest Roman society (Pichon, *Histoire de la littérature latine,* p. 930), made himself the collaborator of King Theodoric, seeking to use his position to instill in the Goths more gentleness and humanity. The king became suspicious and Boethius paid for his failure with his liberty and his life. When he turns to meditations upon the vanity of fortune and power and upon the role of Providence, we can see better today that it was more than classical reminiscence, and we are more willing to overlook his rather annoying allegorizing (though we must admit that he was better in this respect than Martianus Capella in his *Nuptials of Mercury and Philology* of an earlier century in which we already find this tendency so dear to the Middle Ages). This last echo of Platonic thought is the more moving in that it comes from the solitude of a prison.

For the Middle Ages (which offered abundant comment upon the *Consolation* while waiting for its translation into the vernacular), Boethius was also the translator and commentator of the *Ysagoge* of Porphyrius and the interpreter of Aristotelian thought. The medieval schools were to subsist on these writings until the twelfth century, when Aristotle was rediscovered. Four short treatises, particularly the *De Trinitate,* make Boethius "one of the initiators of theological speculation."

As to Cassiodorus (c. 480-570) we scarcely remember that he was the editor of the *Historia Tripartita*. This work offers us only a linguistic interest since historians prefer to go directly to the Greek texts. The some 500 letters which he left us (*Variae*) are representative of the taste of the age. Those from books VI and VII, whose addresses had been omitted, were already *Formulae,* that is, models which the Middle Ages would use extensively.[3] The *Institutiones,* on the other hand, are more than a book. The time was past when one could think, as Cassiodorus himself once had done, of creating at Rome a catholic university modeled on those of Alexandria or Nisibis. Renouncing the high positions which he had occupied, he retired with a small community of monks to his property of Vivarium in Calabria. The *Institutiones* are the charter of this community. Cassiodorus outlines in them a course of study as well as a rule of life. Transplanting into Italy the studious traditions of the Greek monasteries and the schools of the Orient, they created an atmosphere propitious to ancient culture which could survive, though attenuated, and be transmitted to future generations. Each person at Vivarium busied himself according to his means. Those who were little talented for studies could find in Gargilius Martialis and Columella the principles of husbandry and gardening. But for those who had the ability he recommended above all the copying of manuscripts. It was in rereading the sacred books that they would sanctify their souls, and from their transcribing the teachings of the Lord,

[3] Best known are those of Marculf, composed c. 650. Joubert *(lettre à M. de Fontanes du* 5-XI-1794) does them too much honor by placing them among the "books written by old men who knew how to endow them with the originality of their character and age" after Homer, Aeschylus and Varro.

Satan would receive as many wounds as the number of words which the scribe set down. This work, it is true, has no value unless it is accurate, and that is why we must have recourse to the ancient grammarians who treated of orthography. Cassiodorus himself composed a *De Orthographia,* a compendium of the ancient doctrine on the subject. Not content with attending to the quality of the text, he also gave attention to the outward appearance of the volumes. Here we find outlined the program of activity of the Scriptoria of the monasteries of the Middle Ages, and here we see how it happened that the most bitter adversaries of pagan literature were the ones who left the door ajar for the grammarians who, in turn, allowed the whole profane literature to enter after them.

The Rule of Saint Benedict, somewhat older than the *Institutiones,* should be mentioned here, first as a monument to the Latinity of this period, but especially because of its influence. It is not a question of that intellectual work which was to make so many Benedictine abbeys famous. The elaboration of a wise and harmonious rule of life, banishing all excess and giving a place to manual labor as well as to the *lectio divina* (canonical hours) created an atmosphere favorable to the flowering of intellectual activity; a harmony which in the midst of troubled centuries made a privileged world of an abbey.

Isidore of Seville (570-636) was born in that Visigothic Spain in which (once the first wave of invaders had passed) the old guard tried to reorganize the city around the barbarian kings. He towered over all those who maintained the cult of ancient letters (the king Sisebuth, the bishop Braulion, Ildefonsus of Toledo) through the success of one of his works: the *Etymologies* or *Origines*. Save for the Scriptures, there was no other book which enjoyed such a wide circulation in the Middle Ages. It is found in all the libraries, and from it most of the writers, during more than eight centuries, were to draw their knowledge of antiquity. Such success amazes us, in view of the fact that the book was actually a rather mediocre compilation. The etymologies make us smile: *NAVIM quidam perhibent dictam, eo quod* gnavum *rectorem quaerat . . .; AGER latine appelari dicitur, eo quod in eo* agatur *aliquid . . .; VILLA a* vallo, *id est aggere terrae nuncupata, quod pro limite constitui solet* . . . It was all that a still rudimentary science of language could do, but poetry and rhetoric were to find in it a method of development which was widely used. Generally, the encyclopedia thus formed responded adequately to the trend which made of the Middle Ages an age of the Summae and the Specula Mundi; a trend which finds its explanation in the fact that Isidore himself was always conscious of having been born in a period of crisis and would always feel the need of gathering together the little which had escaped the disaster. Into the chapters of his book, Isidore had put antiquity in its entirety; christianized, no doubt, but with its gods, its institutions, its knowledge of animals, plants and minerals, its rhetoric and grammar, its *mirabilia* which were to make naïve centuries (unspoiled from the point of view of information) dream of it as of a paradise lost.

If a Boethius, a Cassiodorus or an Isidore turned toward the past to try to carry away with one last look something of the world which was crumbling behind them, Gregory the Great (540-604) went forward to face the future without regret. He decided, in the same way as the great Doctor, the debate which is illustrated by allegory in the famous dream of S. Jerome.⁴ Supposing that the "Ciceronian or Christian" dilemma was well put, the consequences of the choice revealed themselves as more grave than S. Jerome had imagined. For him it was an affair of individual salvation, but in the age of Gregory the Great it was the fate of all culture which hung in the balance. It is certainly fine to see him refuse to subject the word of God to the rules of Donatus (cf. Migne, P. L. 75, 5, 6). He who had the benefit of a patrician education could permit himself the luxury of disdaining the humble rules of grammar. He did not see what Cassiodorus had sensed by intuition: that the Church, having to conserve and to transmit the text of the sacred Scriptures, had to stand ground with philology and consequently with grammar and ancient letters; that the teaching of the Church rested on Latin; and that Latin (since the standard of usage became increasingly unstable from day to day) rested on Donatus.

This man, who professed an absolute disdain for correctness of language, evidently attached little importance to literary things unless he saw in them a means of action. We shall but mention briefly his *Moralia in Job,* his *Homilies,* his *Liber Regulae Pastoralis,* and even the *Registrum* of his letters, in spite of the interest which such a correspondence would hold from the historical and documentary point of view. We must say a word, however, about his *Dialogi* which were written at Rome in the first years of his pontificate and which immediately experienced a great popularity. We mention them, first because, dealing with *"De Vita et Miraculis Patrum . . . Italicorum,"* they belong to a genre which we

⁴ Labriolle, *History and Literature of Christianity,* p. 26.

meet here for the first time: hagiography; and especially because his view of the world is that which was to prevail during the whole of the first part of the Middle Ages. We feel here an obsession with the idea of an approaching catastrophe (Migne, P. L. 75, 511) in which the supernatural intervenes constantly, and in which the struggle between God and the devil is enacted before the eyes of a horror-stricken humanity.

Some like to envisage Fortunatus as the first, chronologically speaking, of the poets of the Middle Ages; others, as the last representative of ancient letters. In Gaul, this Italian undoubtedly appeared as the ambassador of Roman culture. He took up the role of those "graeculi," rhetoricians or poetasters of whom, eight centuries earlier, the Romans of the Republic had spoken with disdain. But as always, the charm worked and the half barbarian conquerors were visibly flattered to see to what length this representative of a decadent civilization was going. It is painful to see a Roman apply all the resources of his language, his superlative and hyperbole of rhetoric, and still further belittle the indisputable glories of the past in order to celebrate a Duke Lupus or a King Childebert.

Certainly this incense was rather strong, and with its systematic alliteration, the verse was already of a barbaric making. The Middle Ages were never to show marked delicacy in matters of poetic embellishment, and Fortunatus in this case appears as a precursor.[5]

He was born in Treviso, between 530 and 540, and was educated in the celebrated schools of Ravenna. Cured of an affection of his eyesight by the intercession of Saint Martin

[5] We find in his verses such asyndeta as: blanditur, refovet, veneratur, honorat, obumbrat.

he vowed to make a pilgrimage to Tours. Taking the route of the wandering scholars (which tempted some to make him the precursor of the Vagantes) we meet him on the Inn, on the upper Danube, then at Mainz and Cologne. Finally, through Metz, Verdun, Rheims, Soissons and Paris he reached the goal of his journey. Having at last met Queen Radegonde who lived in retirement in a monastery with her adopted daughter, Agnes, the abbess of the convent, he settled at Poitiers. He remained in a charming intimacy with the two nuns for twenty years. "He is a troubadour", says E. K. Rand, "with as deep a devotion as ever knight had for his lady. He used to Queen Radegonde the language of a lover, and his love is rare and pure" (*coelesti affectu, non crimine corporis ullo*).

Fortunatus was never to leave Poitiers after the death of Radegonde, save for a brief trip to the banks of the Moselle. At the end of his life he was elected bishop of his adopted city. He died in 600.

Tired of so many occasional poems, poems of compliment, epithalamiums, epitaphs in which not even the real talent of the verse maker can conceal the emptiness of thought, the reader of today comes upon the pieces dedicated to Metz and to the Moselle with delighted surprise. Is it because the poet here has renounced mythological embellishment in order to describe simply that which he sees before him? Is it because we recognize familiar places? Or is it because, through the Latin lines and from a Europe of so long ago, bleeding from invasions, a man speaks of this countryside which is so dear to us and where we feel everywhere the presence and the work of man? Otherwise, his distichs are monotonous enough, his description scarcely more than enumeration, and some quite charming images occur again and again in poem after poem.

In contrast, a breath of lyric inspiration permeates the *Vexilla regis prodeunt,* written in iambic dimeter with frequent rhyme, and the *Pange Lingua Gloriosi praelium certaminis* (sometimes attributed to Claudianus Mamertinus) in trochaic tetrameters, the meter of the marching songs of the Roman soldiers. Composed upon the occasion of the reception of relics from the True Cross at the monastery of Poitiers, they are still sung (with some unfortunate alterations): the first at the service of Holy Friday, the second during Passion Week.

Different writings in prose: letters, Lives of Saints, (including a Life of S. Radegonde) should be mentioned here because they provide the first examples of real rhymed prose.

Until then, rhyme (*Gleichformreim*) bore upon words which syntactic parallelism (extolled since Gorgias by the theoreticians of art-prose) affected with an identical termination. With Fortunatus the homophony no longer necessarily resulted from grammatical symmetry (*Mischformreim*). We will see, for example, *virginum* rhyme with *collegium* and *dolori* with *contristari*. We are at a turning point in the history of Latin prose.

The impression of Gaul which Fortunatus has left us is that of a happy country, where the great were patrons of letters, where there was room for a life of pleasant society and for quasi-bourgeois virtues, where the echoes of the massacres and horrors of war (*De excidio Thoringiae*) outside only created a greater appreciation of the peace at home. Fortunatus is certainly not a liar: even in the most somber ages, life continues and dispenses its joys, but one feels them more intensely then than in normal times. However, an innate opportunism caused him to turn his eyes away from horrors he did not wish to see. His picture of Gaul must be corrected by that of his contemporary and correspondent, Gregory of Tours (538-593). His *Historia Francorum* is full of accounts of abuses and cruelties of all kinds for which the country daily provided the stage. Belonging to a senatorial family of Clermont-Ferrand, he had been elected bishop of Tours in 573. We know the role which the bishops played in the Gaul of his day. He was the defender of his church and community, energetic and prudent. In constant intercouse with the princes who disputed the possession of the country, he was in a good position to recount the events in which he was involved. He certainly had none of the qualities which we require of a historian today. He was not unbiased; he was credulous, and at any moment would be carried away by his taste for anecdote; the over-all picture apparently did not interest him, but "his naïvité itself (De Ghellinck I, 38), his gift as a narrator, his candid loyalty, give an especial charm and animation to the accounts of affairs in which he was personally concerned." He is also a source of prime importance for historians of this confused epoch. His prose certainly was destitute of art, but in that age it meant that it was also innocent of artifice, and it had the merit of not forcing its presence upon the reader. The place where the reader, trained to the Latin of Cicero and Caesar, will come to grief is with the language: the confusion of genders, of cases, of *suus* and of *eius,* the use of the accusative and the nominative absolute, such constructions as *metuo quod . . . dico tibi quia* (of which we already find isolated cases at the end of the Empire) were from then on common coin, and examples of the dissolution of the language of the upper classes. The schools were closed, and a language which was used now only by a small minority was powerless to furnish that solid norm which Malherbe found again in listening to the porters of Port au Foin. We should note that Gregory of Tours was the first to take account of the situation for which he blamed the troubles of the times.

It was the same with Fortunatus, and other Christian writers before him; but the protestations of humility, which until then were just a form of style or an expression of real sentiment, now became the manifestation of an inferiority complex which was to affect so many writers of the Middle Ages. This complex can be recognized in the apologies of a type which we have just seen; and in the tours de force (such as acrostics and emblematic poems) with which the writers of the Carolingian period insisted on demonstrating their learned taste. But what was later a lack of assurance in using a language learned only in school, is still with Gregory of Tours the feeling of insufficient training, a consequence of the troubled times. One must have very little sense of historical reality, or be very insensitive to the charms of a lively and engaging narration to hold Gregory to strict account for his Latin. His naïveté as an historian is worth its price, in contrast to the certainly more ambitious works which subsequent centuries were to produce. The chronicle of the Pseudo-Fredegar[6] comprises four books of which only the last is original. We recognize in it the hands of several successive authors (the last one around the year 660).

[6] *Pseudo* because the name derives from the misreading of *sed carius*> *Fredcarius*>*Fredegarius*.

The *Liber Historiae Francorum* was written in its main portions by a Frank from Neustria (c. 727), but was not finished until ten years later. The prologue of the fourth book of the Pseudo-Fredegar sets down the unrest of a powerless witness to the disintegration of ancient civilization.

The importance of these two works lies in the fact that they are the source of the legend of the Trojan origin of the Franks. "An erudite legend, fabricated entirely by learned persons," says E. Champeaux who investigated the old Alsatian versions of the legend where shrewdness and ignorance go hand in hand to produce a work of political and juridical propaganda; for these legends had the tendency to provide the barbaric people with a title of nobility comparable to that of the Romans and to justify the pretensions of their rulers.

The contrast between the ignorance which Gregory of Tours or the Pseudo-Fredegar deplore, and the philological erudition of Virgil the Grammarian is of the kind which is apparent in all ages of decadence. The identity of that namesake of the great poet is still enigmatic. Only one late source designates him as being from Toulouse. In any case he was a Gaul, probably from Bigorre. There is still more doubt about the period in which he lived. He has been placed anywhere from the fifth to the ninth centuries, but certain indications lead us to put him at the end of the sixth century. He has left us *Epitomae* (fifteen essays on questions of grammar in the broader sense of the word) and *Epistolae* (letters on the eight parts of speech). The approach to these works is difficult. Their Latin was not only subject to the influence of the spoken language of the period, it was not only enriched by elements of Hebrew, Greek and Celtic, but carried with it also the inventions of the school of Toulouse. Did that esoteric language represent a real state of learning? Was it the work of an imposter? The Abbé Tardi, in the preface of his French translation of the *Epitomae* (Paris, 1928) certainly comes very near to the truth with the suggestion that he was "a vain provincial, dazzled and fanaticized by the teachers of his small town," as does Lejay who speaks of "a soul where barbaric atmosphere, scholastic tradition, naïve curiosity and pedantic puerility are strangely mingled." We would not dwell upon the case of Virgilius Maro the Grammarian if his teachings had not founded a school and if we were not going to encounter his influence presently.

While, in the old provinces of the Western Empire, the language and civilization of Rome were either entirely annihilated (as in Africa and Spain), or well on the way of disintegration (as in Gaul), there arose, as through a kind of miracle, a new home of Latin culture outside of the Roman World. Ireland had learned Latin only through the missionaries who came to evangelize, and probably also "thanks to Gallic refugees during the period of the Hun and Gothic invasions." But the Irish monks did not content themselves with the rudiments. They did not turn away from the profane authors, says Roger,[7] being afraid neither of reviving paganism (the Greek and Roman gods were a matter of indifference to them) nor of sacrificing faith to rhetoric, as the use of rustic Latin by the faithful did not, as on the continent, lead to further departure from classical standard. On the other hand, Ireland in the sixth century remained safely aloof from the convulsions which shook the rest of Europe. For her, on the contrary, it was an age of great pros-

---

[7] *L'Enseignement des Lettres Classiques d'Ausone à Alcuin*, p. 229.

perity for the monastic schools. Several good manuscripts attribute to St. Columba (died 597) the founder of Iona or
Hy on the western coast of Scotland (not to be confused with
St. Columban, the founder of Bobbio), the *"Altus Prosator"*
(i. e., Creator) which is used as a hymn by the Irish Church.
In any case it is one of the first poetic productions of Ireland. It is written in iambic dimeter, accentual and rhyming,
and it tells in 23 alphabetical strophes the complete history
of the world from the Creation to the Last Judgment. Its
powerfully compressed evocations recall the frescoes of S.
Savin, while the last strophes show how the Vulgate text of
the prophet Zephaniah is at the source of the tradition which
leads to the *Dies Irae*. The reader's attention is arrested by
strange terms: Hellenisms, words drawn from the glossaries.
We will presently find them again in the *Hisperica Famina*.
The really Irish pieces in the *Bangor Antiphonary* (preserved in Bobbio and passed on to the Ambrosiana in Milan)
and those of the Irish *Liber Hymnorum* present some characteristic features: rhythm founded on the number of syllables rather than on accent, alliteration and frequently rich
two-syllable rhymes, features which already forshadow, says
Raby (Christian Latin Poetry, p. 138), the poetry of Hildebert and of Adam of S. Victor.

The Celtic enthusiasm for moving about and traveling
which made adventurous pilgrims and prodigious dissemina-
tors of the faith of the Irish monks, had led St. Columba
into Scotland; it was to lead St. Columban (540-615) to the
continent, where he would found Luxeuil and Bobbio. He
too, in his way, was a writer: we owe to him the first metrical
poems of Irish origin.

In Great Britain, the Saxon Conquest had pushed back to

the south and to the west what remained of the Church, the last mainstay of Latin civilization on the islands after the retreat of the Roman legions. There it was, toward the middle of the sixth century, that Gildas wrote in an abstruse and artless prose his *De Excidio et Conquestu Britanniae,* rather a bitter pamphlet than an historical narrative. He says that he had to go overseas in search of his sources of information, as the native sources were either destroyed or dispersed by the invaders. If he is the author of the *Lorica* (the manuscript reads: *Gillus hanc Loricam fecit ad demones expellendos*), he must have been familiar with the background from which the *Hisperica Famina* came, since they were also influenced by the grammatical theories of Virgil of Toulouse. The strangeness of this exorcism makes the work almost untranslatable. Its structure consists of rhythmic verse of eleven syllables, rhyming, if one can call homophony of the last syllable a rhyme, and consequently non-accentual.

The *Hisperica Famina* (Hisperic sayings or words, that is, Irish, although they too originated in the Southwest of Great Britain) are a rather short work. They contain, in a kind of rhythmic prose, a series of elaborations on various subjects: on study, the use of time, the elements of the universe, sky, water, fire, wind, etc. Perhaps they were school exercises. Their vocabulary is composite: we can distinguish the elements peculiar to classical language, to Church Latin, Vulgar Latin, transcriptions of Greek or Hebrew words, derivations by means of the suffix *men* or *eus;* and eventually, as though these resources were still not sufficient, terms whose descent from any known language has not been established. The phraseology is short, abrupt, and though it has few subordinate clauses, it is obscured by an abuse of epithets and paraphrases.

The re-evangelization of Great Britain, undertaken in 597 by St. Augustine of Canterbury, was to prepare the way for the restoration of study; but the restoration did not really begin until 70 years later when the Pope sent to the island Theodore of Tarsus who had studied at Athens, and Hadrian, an African who had dedicated himself to theology. They had the mission to reorganize the English Church, but their role as educators was no less important. Bede (*Hist. Eccl.* IV, 2) notes that "even today, one can find some of their disciples who know Latin and Greek as if it were their mother tongue." While Canterbury was becoming a center of study, an Anglo-Saxon, Benedict Biscop, after having been at Rome and having visited the abbeys of the continent, founded two monasteries at Wearmouth and at Jarrow in the region of Newcastle. The first Anglo-Saxon man of letters is Aldhelm (c. 640-709) of royal descent, a pupil of Hadrian at Canterbury, later a monk, and Abbot of Malmesbury. In prose, at least when he had the time to cultivate his style, he used a pompous language, strongly influenced by the *Hisperica Famina,* abounding in abstract words, hellenisms, and full of alliterations, which was the reason for the severe judgment passed upon him by Taine (Litt. Angl. I, 67). His hexameters, however, where the discipline of the verse obliged him to use words whose quantity was indicated by the grammarians and poets, are dull. "His faults," says Roger, "are those of an inept age where curiosity was born again after a period of ignorance."

Aldhelm had pupils, one of whom was Aethelwald, King

of Mercia. He was an innovator, and on that count worthy of being cited here. However we now come to a work and to a man who deserves our greater attention. Bede the Venerable was, at the age of seven, entrusted to Benedict Biscop. He studied later under the direction of Ceolfrid his disciple. He was deacon at the age of 19 and priest at 30. From then on until his last breath, the history of his life is identical with that of his work. Nothing outside of it could interrupt his untiring activity. He was an indefatigable commentator of the Sacred Scriptures which he translated into the vernacular. He also was an hagiographer, in prose and in verse. His *Historia Ecclesiastica Gentis Anglorum,* says De Ghellinck (I, p. 62) "is a model of loyalty, sincerity and also of criticism. The union of these qualities was extremely rare in his period." We also owe to him hymns and epigrams, but he was foremost a man of learning. We have the treatise *de Orthographia, de Metrica, de Schematibus* (technique), *de Temporibus, de Natura Rerum,* the fruit of his studies of the ancient authors. "His intercourse with them," says Roger (p. 308), "furnished him not only with some expressions . . . hemistichs here and there in his prose . . . certain descriptive words interpolated into his style . . . but usages of language which correspond to real culture." There is no longer any sterilizing purism. "He considered Latin a living language, and he had no conception of the idea of classical usage in the name of which one could proscribe the imitation of writers such as Fortunatus or St. Augustine." He put himself in their ranks, but at the same time, he avoided all school pedantry. There is, for example, no trace in him of the style of the *Hisperica Famina.* "Bede," concludes Roger (p.

319), "truly came under the influence of the ancients; he owes to them that moderation, that neatness of style which are so rare in his contemporaries and so gratifying after the incoherence of an Aldhelm." In his time, he was admired particularly for his encyclopedic knowledge, and this renown was not to change in the following centuries.

Although he preceded the Carolingian Renaissance by only a short span of time, he deserves to figure, with Boethius, Cassiodorus, Isidore and St. Gregory the Great, among the founders of the Middle Ages.

A complete contrast to his life is that of his contemporary, Wynfreth, better known under the name of St. Boniface (c. 675-754). While the whole existence of the one was passed in scholarly retreat, a missionary zeal tore Wynfreth away from the abbey where he had studied and later taught, and made him the Apostle to the Germans. One of his disciples was to found the famous abbey of Fulda. Boniface himself met with a martyr's death among the Frisians. This man of action was always to keep his veneration for learning. If, like his compatriots, he practiced particularly rhythmic verse of Irish influence, he also left riddles in verse and he even composed elaborate emblematic poems: youthful manifestations of a true love of letters which the Anglo-Saxons cultivated not only for their usefulness, but also for the charm which they add to life.

In any case, "the appearance of the new Anglo-Saxon culture in the seventh century is perhaps the most important event between the age of Justinian and that of Charlemagne."[8]

[8] Ch. Dawson, *The Making of Europe*, p. 206.

Alcuin, the principal artisan of the Carolingian Renaissance, came from the school of York. With him, the heritage of ancient culture is definitely saved from the shipwreck in which it was almost lost forever.

The Carolingian Renaissance

LITERARILY SPEAKING, the most tangible testimony of the rebirth of intellectual activity which we connect with the name of Charlemagne, is found in the four (a fifth is in the making) large quarto volumes of the *Monumenta Germaniae Historica*. A particular section of this famous collection, the *Poetae Aevi Carolini,* reassembles the abundant poetic production, or more exactly, the abundance of versified pieces of this period. One cannot deny the fact that they are generally very unattractive. The evident progress in the correctness of the verse, the virtuosity itself of the verse makers, was very dearly paid for by a regression. What good is a return to ancient models if it is for a purely formal imitation?

Nevertheless, it would be an error to hold to this first impression. It was only a flowering whose luxuriance was deceptive, since it produced nothing but school works. The real fruits were to come much later. The literary aspect of the Carolingian Renaissance, moreover, does not facilitate conclusions as to its origins, or furnish explanations of its outcome.

The capitular *de Scolis* gives an exposé of the leading motives underlying the reform desired by the ruler. Almost illiterate himself (it was said that he learned to write only late in life), Charlemagne appreciated the importance of learning and the necessity of a sound education for those to whom he entrusted the spiritual and material welfare of his people.

[27]

Later, reasons of prestige led this emperor of Germanic origin to surround himself with writers who knew Latin. Like Theodoric before him, he wanted to be the continuator of the traditions of Rome. An innovation of a smaller character was to have such great consequences that it could be compared to the invention of printing: It was the substitution of the so-called "Carolingian minuscule" for the characters of writing employed until then.

As a corollary, the *Scriptoria* of the monasteries entered upon a period of activity which was to contribute greatly to the growth and dissemination of libraries. Libraries had been almost nonexistent in the West. The Apostolical Library in Rome, the libraries of Bobbio and of York—those were almost the only ones we could find. What had become of those of Visigothic Spain? Now, in addition to the libraries at Tours, Corbie, S. Riquier, Lorsch, Fulda, St. Gall, Reichenau, S. Emmeran—there were soon to be libraries at S. Wandrille, Bec, Cluny, S. Amand, Durham, Bamberg, Pruefening. In spite of the destructions wrought by the Norman invasions, the movement was not to be stopped. Of course, those libraries scarcely resembled those of our day.[1] Our great depositories count their volumes by the hundreds of thousands and the more important ones exceed the million mark. Bobbio in the tenth century, which owned 660 volumes was an exception. The monastic libraries of the High Middle Ages that counted more than five hundred volumes were rare indeed. On the other hand, we should always note, as De Ghellinck points out, that the old catalogues appear to indicate the title of the volume rather than its detailed contents,

---

[1] On this subject, see the two articles of De Ghellinck in *Nouvelle Revue Théologique,* January and February, 1938.

so that it might be correct to double or triple the given figures in order to obtain the actual number of works. Another important consideration is that the libraries were used in an entirely different way. Our libraries constitute an enormous mass of rich documentation, for users who consult for reference, rather than read, the books. The medieval monk, however, not only read his book, but studied it, meditated upon it, when he was not transcribing it. The rarity of the works alone was a reason (at least during the epochs and in the centers where studies were held in honor) for extracting from them all their substance. Seen this way, the radiation of the centers of study of which we have spoken, becomes less astonishing. They all issued directly or indirectly from the great intellectual renewal desired by Charlemagne; and the first home of this renewal was the great emperor's court itself.

Among those who constituted the small circle dedicated to the cultivation of letters (and with what youthful earnestness they went about it we may guess it from the fictitious names they gave themselves: Homer, Naso, Pindar, Menalcas . . .) the only one who is really known is Alcuin (735-804). Here posterity has judged rightly in remembering the name of the man, but not the titles of his works, for this great scholar and organizer, "the first intellectual among Charlemagne's officials" (Guizot) and "one of the men to whom Western Civilization owes most" (Gilson)—was only a second-rate writer.

A good portion of his poetical work has only an historical value for us, such as the *Versus de Patribus, regibus et sanctis Euboricensis ecclesiae,* devoted to the program of studies and the library of his abbey in York. Its classical reminiscenses give evidence of a return to the great models (especially Virgil, but also Ovid and Lucan). As for Horace, Alcuin can have known him only through quotation, although he choose Flaccus for his surname. A subject such as the destruction of the monastery of Lindisfarne lent itself to variations upon the inconsistency of fortune, a favorite theme of the Middle Ages. His work also comprises hymns, lives of saints, and many occasional poems. They show the progress made in the technique of versification. Some have a real charm, such as the "Farewell to his Cell" which makes us wonder whether we see here a true feeling for nature, or rather a remembrance of things read.

We may mention here (although there is a tendency to attribute it to an unknown Irishman) the *Debate between Spring and Winter* which Virgilian shepherds are called upon to arbitrate: they decide in favor of Spring which brings back the cuckoo, the traditional messenger of the renewal of life in northern lands (might this not be an influence of song or folktale?). This poem is one of the first examples of a literary genre (*Conflictus*) that was to be developed greatly in the centuries to come.

Paul the Deacon was, as Peter of Pisa and Paulinus of Aquileia, a Lombard. He attached himself to Charlemagne after the destruction of the kingdom of Didier. The epanaleptic[2] lines in which he celebrates Lake Como are not without charm, but it is a charm which doubtless depends more upon the evocation of an incomparable site than upon the genius of the poet. Moreover, his literary reminiscences too

[2] This term means distichs in which the first half of the hexameter is repeated by the second half of the pentameter. These were in great vogue during the Middle Ages.

often take the place of inspiration (cf. *Quam tuus e nostro labatur pectore vultus,* V. 19).

An *Alfabetum de bonis sacerdotibus prosa compositum,* which the editors place at the end of his poems, has a counterpart in the *Alfabetum de malis sacerdotibus,* in which certain verses already have the mark of the goliardic satires.

Finally, though on the faith of late evidence, the learned hymnologist G. M. Dreves attributes to Paul the Deacon the famous hymn to St. John the Baptist:

> UT *queant laxis* REsonare *fibris*
> MIra *gestorum* FAmuli *tuorum*
> SOLve *polluti* LAbii *reatum*
>   *Sancte Johannes.*

Guido of Arezzo gave this verse to his pupils to help them remember the tones of the scale, and it is from this verse that the notes were named. As it was in Alcuin's case, poetry for Paul the Deacon was only one aspect—the most imaginative, but also the most superficial—of a literary activity whose most notable remains is a *Historia Langobardorum,* written at Monte Cassino. It is extremely precious to us because of his position at the court of the last Lombard princes, and has additional interest through the inclusion of national legends and of popular tradition. Linguists are grateful to him for having preserved for us a compendium of the lexicographer Festus. He was also the compiler of the great Carolingian Book of Homilies, composed at Charlemagne's order and dedicated to him.

Theodulph (c. 760-821), a Visigoth from the north of Spain, was educated in the schools where the traditions of the time of Isidore of Seville were perpetuated; at the Palace

Academy he bore the name of Pindar, and he was considered the most important poet of his epoch. He had read the Christian poets, Prudentius in particular, and among the pagan writers Pompey (the historian Trogus Pompeius?), Donatus, Virgil, and Ovid. Under the lightheartedness of their fables are found many truths, he said: a theory which one meets many times in the course of the Middle Ages, and which justifies the allegorical exegeses of the "Ovides Moralisés." Appointed to the episcopal seat of Orleans, he was, in 798, *missus dominicus,* and his tour of inspection gave us a long piece, full of curious details about the countries through which he traveled and about the judiciary customs of the day. If the passage from the *ad Carolum Regem,* where the emperor is welcomed by his daughters, is quoted so often:

> *Berta rosas, Chrodtrudh violas dat, lila Gisla,*
> *Nectaris ambrosii praemia quaeque ferat;*
> *Rothaid poma, Hiltrudh Cererem, Tetdrada Liaeum*

(it resembles a verse from the *Latin Anthology,* Riese 393, 8), is that not an admission that it is one of the only passages in these long poems where we can find something beyond mere documentary interest?

There is, however, a true lyricism and overtones of a fine inspiration in his *Gloria laus et honor tibi sit rex Christe redemptor,* from which the processional hymn still sung on Palm Sunday was taken. The hymn immediately became popular, and a charming legend asserts that Theodulph, fallen into disgrace and imprisoned after the death of Charlemagne, owed to it his liberty and his pardon.

With Angilbert, we come to the only member of the Palace Academy who was of Frankish origin. The others whom we have mentioned so far were Anglo-Saxons, Lombards and Spanish Goths. There also is Modoin (Naso) of unknown origin of whose work little has survived. Angilbert was a disciple of Alcuin, and his talents designated him for the important missions for which the emperor rewarded him by making him lay abbot of Saint- Riquier. From his union with Bertha, daughter of Charlemagne, he had two sons. One of them, Nithard, was the historian of the sons of Louis the Pious. Angilbert had a violent temperament, and Alcuin on two occasions expresses fear of his passion for the stage-players, spectacles and other *diabolica figmenta*. As a poet (Homer in the little court circle) he left us scarcely anything (if we must deny him the *Karolus Magnus et Leo Papa* of which we will speak later) save the *Ecloga ad Karolum Regem* where there is enough intensity of feeling to make us forget the paucity of the subject.

In the first rank of the men of the second Carolingian generation we must cite Raban Maur (784-856), disciple of Alcuin at Tours, scholar, later Abbot of Fulda, finally Bishop of Mainz. He merits the title of "teacher of Germany." We will bypass his work as exegetist, grammarian, encyclopaedist and moralist: it has nothing to do with his originality. He studied versification with Alcuin: it was from then on one of the requisites of a good education. We can thus understand why so many poems were destined to be forgotten. Irish models influenced a great rhythmic poem on the Catholic faith, of which a good part was an imitation of the *Altus Prosator*. Certain manuscripts (of contested authority) put the *Veni Creator* under the name of Raban. The famous hymn is in any case a production of the Carolingian Renaissance.

In the western part of the empire, Hincmar of Rheims (d. 882) occupied a place comparable to that of Raban in the eastern part. He must have been the continuator of the *Annales Sancti Bertini,* for a historian of merit was there revealed. He could speak from first hand knowledge, since he had taken part in the dynastic rivalries as well as in the theological quarrels which stirred his century.

Walafrid Strabo (809-849), disciple of Raban, is along with him one of the most typical representatives of the culture of the great German abbeys of the first half of the ninth century. He came of an obscure family, but his talents destined him, at the age of twenty, to be the tutor of the future Charles the Bald. He eventually became abbot of Reichenau which he had entered as a monk, and he died by accident at the age of forty, in the course of a mission to his former pupil.

He was remarkably precocious and had, at eighteen, put into verse the account of the visions which his master Wettin had had before dying and which had transported him from hell to purgatory and to paradise. Walafrid gives, as it were, a first sketch of the *Divine Comedy.* We leave aside the *De Imagine Tetrici,* a panegyric of Louis the Pious and of the imperial family. It is the *De Cultura Hortorum* (better known under the name *Hortulus*) which makes Walafrid so appealing. Following the model of Columella and of the Pseudo-Apuleius (*De Herbarum Virtutibus*), but yet original, he leads us into the little garden to which he consecrated his hours of leisure at Reichenau. He bids us halt before the chervil, the poppy, the wild celery, the betony, the horse-radish, the sage, of whose dietetic and therapeutic virtues he tells us. He finishes with the rose, symbol of the blood of the martyrs, and with the lily, reward of the saints. Walafrid's skill as a versifier was great. He knew how to handle the most diverse lyric metres, but instead of making his virtuosity show, he contented himself very simply with hexameters. This simplicity, so well in accord with the subject, is an additional charm. Perhaps we see in the verses of the monk of Reichenau a little too much of the naïveté of a Francis Jammes: such an avatar happens, after all, only to a work which lasts. The *Hortulus* is still read and translated, not for scientific purposes, but for pleasure. André Thérive and a distinguished botanist, Henri Leclerc, have but recently tried. Remy de Gourmont who cites several verses in *Le Latin Mystique* showed them how it should not be translated:

> *Sic mea sic fragili de stirpe cucurbita surgens*
> *Diligit appositas, sua sustentacula, furcas.*

"My frail (?) . . . but his text gives fragilis . . . pumpkin in growing adores the sustentacular forks (!) affixed under its flexibility (!!!)."

The Irish, however, continued to come in great numbers to the continent, for their learning opened all doors for them. However, their strange mode of behavior made others look at them askance. *"Sottish-Scots:"* the pun is ready, and Theodulph lays stress upon it in connection with the Irish admitted to the court of Charlemagne. Clement the grammarian and Smaragdus, perhaps, were Scots, and the *Hibernicus exul,* who addressed verses to the emperor, has been identified as a Dungal by Traube, as Dicuil by Esposito. At the beginning of the ninth century a certain Colmanus finds, in an epistle in verse, almost Virgilian language to say farewell to his namesake who had the good fortune to return to his distant homeland.

John Scotus Erigena, "the first really great name in medieval philosophy" (E. Gilson), was upon occasion a poet. Toward 847, he was in Paris at the court of Charles the Bald to whom he addressed Greek verses. His Latin poems were, moreover, stuffed with derived words or words simply translated from the Greek. For our purposes, we must dwell at greater length upon another Irishman, Sedulius Scotus: first because he is one of the best poets of his time; then because since he was at Liège between 848 and 858 (after which date we lose trace of him); it is with him that the Belgian provinces really enter into the history of letters. Previously, they had yielded scarcely anything but a *Vita* and *Miracula Sancti Remacli* at Stavelot and a *Vita S. Huberti* at Liège. Henri Pirenne who has devoted his first publication[3] to our poet, tells how the poor traveler arrived in the Belgian country in a snow storm with two compatriots, grammarians like himself. Bishop Hartgar furnished first a more than modest abode such as would be offered, probably, to vagabonds. Sedulius soon made himself known by his accomplished flattery and especially by his more real talents which made him indispensable. Liège, where he found "the quiet favorable to studies, the leisure which permitted him agreeable relaxation . . . good friends . . . and listeners who refused him neither applause nor recompense," became his adopted country. Sedulius—we may read between the lines of hyperbolic

[3] *Mémoires couronnés de l'Académie.* XXXIII, 1882, 8.

praise which he addressed to his benefactor—seems to have felt profound gratitude and affection for Hartgar. After Hartgar's death, it is true, he hailed the coming of his successor, Franco de Lobbes, in terms equally dithyrambic. This is a flaw of court poets in general; but here it was aggravated by a weakness which we find often in the Latin poets of the Middle Ages: their sentiments, however sincere, could be expressed only by conventional means. This fear of differing from sacred models paralyzed them, particularly when it was necessary to maintain an elevated tone. Thus we appreciate only Sedulius' works of simple and homely inspiration and those where, instead of the pedant preoccupied with showing his knowledge of meter and mythology, we see the man. To the pomposity of such a beginning:

> *Florida Thespiadum soror ac praenobilis Eglae*
> *Cignea, mellifluos nunc cane, posco, tropos;*
> *Obsecro: Pegaseo flavum caput erige fonte,*
> *Femina doctiloquax organicumque decus;*
> *Syrmate purpureo glaucisque venusta capillis,*
> *Oscula de labiis Sedulio roseis....*

we prefer the verses in which he paints himself, reading or writing, spending his time in teaching, meditation and prayer, invoking the muses in his poetry, admitting his weaknesses . . . he was a man who loved good food and drink and slept soundly. He also employs his talents to picture for us, in high-flown style, the misery in which he and his companions are thrown: They are hungry; moreover, being used to wine, they cannot acquire a taste for the beer of the country. Two lines added later show that the expected result had been obtained: the good Hartgar had laughed and paid. A piece in the same vein addressed to a certain Robert:

Rot—bone, sint nobis per te solacia—berte

(this strange method of practising tmesis was not peculiar to Sedulius) was worth three hundred bottles of wine to the "Scottigenae," more than they had dared hope for!

We have perhaps dwelt too much upon Sedulius; a little because he is a Belgian by adoption; but especially because there appear with him several traits which a few centuries later so clearly defined goliardic poetry. We have considered the theme of the poor poet's lamentation, his lack of shame in holding out his palm. Add to this his praise of good wine, the *Natureingang* (but what poet has not sung of spring?) his impatience with bad pastors, his taste for irreverent parody, his techniques which became common in the twelfth century. All this, we must admit, reveals itself only to the patient eye of erudite analysis,[4] being drowned in laborious and stilted verse.

How much more touching are the accents which Gottschalk found, in exile, to answer a young cleric who asked him for some verses. Is it the tenderness of the diminutives: *pusiole, filiole, miserule;* the music of the rhythm (two iambic lines followed by two trochaic); or is it the obsessive rhyme in "e" throughout the ten stanzas? Is it the sadness which one feels pierces the simplicity of these lines? "Our sweetest songs are those that tell of saddest thought." We must go back to the finest epoch of classic Latinity to find, with different music, accents as poignant.

---

[4] See Boris Jarcho, *Die Vorlaeufer des Golias,* Speculum III, 1928, p. 523 ff.

Gottschalk (c. 805-869) had been, at Fulda and under Raban, the companion at study and friend of Walafrid Strabo; but the monastic discipline lay heavily upon him and he asked to be released from his vows. Thence came conflicts with his superiors, in which he inevitably came out the worse, which were aggravated when at Orbais and then at Hautvillers he began to preach and write upon the question which became the stumbling block of so many disquieted souls: that of predestination. He was hounded until his death. The bitterness of his enemies had strengthened him in his pride; and Hincmar could note, with a harshness which followed his adversary to the other side of the grave, that his death had been worthy of his life, and that he had gone where he must go—*et abiit in locum suum.* However, when his theological treatises no longer offer us anything but a retrospective interest, the verses in which we feel the distress of an unhappy soul can still move us. Is he the author of the famous eclogue entitled *Theodolus* (*Theo - doulos -* Gottschalk) where, for the edification of countless generations of students, the shepherdess Alithia places the narratives of the Old Testament in opposition to the mythological fables sung by the shepherd Pseustis? Osternacher says yes and Strecker says no; it matters little in any case: Gottschalk's fame is not there.

After him, his contemporaries, a Florus of Lyon, a Paulus Albarus (a converted Jew of Spain), a Milo of S. Amand and a Mico of S. Riquier, deserve only mention. The *Ecloga de Calvis,* dedicated to Charles the Bald, is a praise of baldness and of illustrious baldheads, in 146 hexameters in which all words begin with the letter c. This poem gained for Hucbald of S. Amand (840-930) a certain kind of celebrity. The education which he received from the learned Heiric d'Auxerre, his Lives of Saints in verse, his *Harmonica Institutio,* his great culture especially, attested to by the list of books which he left to his abbey (many are today the glory of the library of Valenciennes): all these are more worthy titles in the eyes of posterity. But with him, and with Radbod of Utrecht who lived in the literary milieu of the court of Charles the Bald, and who wrote a graceful poem on a swallow, we pass over the border into the tenth century. We must go back somewhat.

Taken altogether, Carolingian poetry manifests a return to the classical. It is a victory of school over illiteracy, but it is also the return to an artificial versification, to a poetry whose public is limited to a small circle of educated people and which rarely escaped pedantry and academicism. Happily, the triumph of metric poetry was not complete. It succeeded in slowing down, no doubt, but not in stopping the fountain of rhythmic or "popular" poetry . . . an unfortunate epithet if it leads one to believe that this poetry burst spontaneously from the depth of the common people. This was the error of the romantics; for such has been the case with no literature, and most certainly not with a literature written in a language which the people no longer spoke. This poetry, however, was popular in the sense that it was no longer based upon the quantity of the syllables (which idea belongs only to those who have struggled at school with the theoretical treatises), in that it can be sung equally as well as songs in the vulgar language and that the simplicity of its syntax and of its vocabulary make it sufficiently intelligible to an unlettered public. Thus we see that in writing the hymns which were for the use of the multitude of the faithful, the poets often exhibited a predilection for rhythmic verse. Alcuin himself, according to Strecker, must have composed some (cf. the three pieces edited in *Monumenta, Poetae Kar. Aevi,* IV, 903, ff.).

The same anxiety to share with the people in praise of a hero or in lamentation for a bereavement or a misfortune also made writers prefer rhythmic poetry for compositions in which we perceive the germinal seed of the future *chansons de geste.* The temptation to go back as far as possible is great, but the documents are so scattered and so poor that they inevitably give birth to hypotheses and theories. Such is the case, for example, with the famous cantilena cited by Hildegarius, in his *Life of S. Faron.*

Hildegarius, in 869, recounted events of the two preceding centuries. What documents did he employ? Where did he find the text of his cantilena? The expression *juxta rusticitatem* which he uses in this connection might apply to this barbaric Latin as well as to a song in the vulgar tongue which he would have had to translate in order to introduce it into his tale.

Let us leave this quicksand. Here is, at the end of the eighth century, a complete series of sufficiently long and distinctive pieces to enable us to consider them for themselves, without having to turn to hazardous reconstructions. The campaign against the Avares alone inspired three poems in epic spirit. An unknown author intones a song of triumph in honor of the victorious Prince Pippin, son of Charlemagne. The Lombard grammarian, Paulinus, friend of Alcuin and also connected with the Palace School (Charlemagne was to elevate him to the dignity of Patriarch of Aquileia in 787) is the author of a *planctus* (funeral hymn) in iambic rhythm (fourteen stanzas of five lines) in which he deplores the death of Eric, duke of Friaul, on the battlefield. (799). He wrote, perhaps, another lamentation upon the destruction of Aquileia by the Huns, an historic event to which the menace of the Avares gave a renewed timeliness.

In all probability, it was one of the Irish monks from Bobbio (the invocation *O Columbane* in the seventeenth stanza would seem to indicate this) who wrote the *planctus* on the death of Charlemagne. Its recurring refrain resounds mournfully at the end of twenty stanzas whose brevity does not permit rhetoric to substitute itself for a genuine sentiment.

> *A solis ortu usque ad occidua*
> *littora maris planctus pulsat pectora*
> *Heu mihi misero!*

Another song of lamentation, dictated this time by the horror which a fratricidal struggle inspired, was the *Versus de bella* (battle) *quae fuit acta Fontaneto.* (Fifteen stanzas in alphabetic order, A-P, in three trochaic catalectic tetrameters). Of its author, a certain Angilbert, only what he himself tells us is known, that he was one of the few survivors of the first line of battle. Even in the midst of battle he *observed,* and more especially, was able to transform his observation into words of somber accent:

> *Albent campi vestimenti mortuorum lineis*
> *velut solent in autumno albescere avibus.*

After shuddering at this scene of carnage, the poet ends, as is customary in these lamentations, by asking prayers for those who perished on that fatal day.

One cannot see, for all that, how these pieces could have given birth to an épopée, if the return to the classic models had not awakened vast ambitions, responding to the strong conviction of the men around Charlemagne and their successors that they were the heirs of the Roman Empire. Did not the contemporary events furnish the opportunity for competition with Homer (that is, with the *Ilias Latina*) and with Virgil?

In the *Karolus Magnus et Leo Papa,* which is perhaps Angilbert's, (the Homer of the Palatine school), we find a naive tracing of the ancient épopée. It was the art of an era which incorporated in its edifices the marble and columns taken from the monuments of Rome and Ravenna. Our poet applied himself to paraphrasing rather than to copying; but at times an obvious awkwardness[5] reminds us that he was more faithful to the letter than to the spirit of his model. What must be noted is that he retained the themes which were to become those of the chansons de geste: description of a hunt, with portraits of the king and his suite; recital of a dream, inspired by those in the *Aeneid* and the *Pharsalia*. In sum, the work is not without merit, and sometimes, says Maurice Wilmotte[6] "a breath of real poetry animates the recital and confers upon it a romantic interest; and when Charlemagne addresses his warriors and encourages them to take up their arms again, it is like a fragment of an épopée which has escaped oblivion."

The rôle of the school in the renaissance of epic literature is quite difficult to determine, but was not the *Hague frag-*

---

[5] *Effodiunt portus,* cf. *En.,* I, 427, in the episode on the construction of the palace of Aix-la-Chapelle!

[6] *Origines du Roman en France,* p. 132.

ment (M.G.H., S.S. III, 708) whose prose-hidden verses lent themselves to restoration, thus revised through scholarly labor? There, students of Romance languages find the names of the protagonists of the *Geste de Guillaume d'Orange,* a fact which gives to these few pages an interest which far surpasses their intrinsic value.

It seems that the name alone of Ermoldus Nigellus (Ermold the Dark) exerted its influence upon J. K. Huysmans, who put in the library of Des Esseintes his "poem written in regular hexameters (it is in distichs) in an austere, almost forbidding style and in a Latin of iron dipped in monastic waters, with here and there, a glimpse of sentiment in the hard metal"(!) (*A Rebours,* p. 52.) The poem in question, written to the glory of Louis the Pious by a courtier in disgrace who was desirous of regaining the royal favor, reveals a "rather mediocre writer whose spirit is dry and whose style is poor." At the most, Faral[7] concedes him some fortunate comparisons where he observed in precise fashion (nothing more) "certain scenes of rustic life which excite our imagination more, apparently, than they did his." This chronicle in verse, narrating military expeditions and painting the pomp of the court also forms one of the links which unite the ancient épopée to the chanson de geste.

With the *Waltharius,*[8] we come at last to an original épopée. It transports us to the camp of Attila where three young people, the Frank Hagen, the Burgundian maiden Hildegunde and the Aquitanian Waltharius are held hostage. One day Hagen succeeds in escaping. Some time later, Wal-

---

[7] Preface to his edition in *Classiques de l'Histoire de France,* Vol. XII.
[8] The latest edition of the poem is that by K. Strecker (with German translation by P. Vossen), Berlin 1947.

tharius, taking Hildegunde up behind him in the saddle, also makes his escape. The Huns who had learnt to appreciate the valor of the Aquitanian prince when he fought in their ranks, dare not pursue the fugitives whose flight continues to Worms without hindrance. News of their passage is brought to the court of King Gunther. Hagen guesses that the news is about his companions in exile, but he cannot dissuade the king from launching out in their pursuit, with the hope of seizing upon the treasures which they took with them. Reluctantly, he joins the small band which sets out upon the traces of Waltharius and Hildegunde. Waltharius waits for his adversaries in a pass of the Vosges mountains in the debouchment of a path where two men could not stand side by side. On the first day, he triumphs over all those who risk and attack. The next day at dawn, Gunther and Hagen begin again, but this time Waltharius confronts them in open terrain. All three, finally, are grievously wounded. Waltharius has lost his right hand; Hildegunde dresses their wounds; and reconciled in each other's blood, they return to their native land. Waltharius weds Hildegunde and reigns for a long time. Throughout the length of the one thousand four hundred and fifty lines, the poet succeeds in keeping his reader's close attention, and this even in the midst of the narration of single combats whose recurrence could possibly engender some monotony. We must go back to the text in order to appreciate the profound originality of the work which may be seen beyond the frequent borrowings from Virgil. Questions about the author, country of origin and epoch which gave us the *Waltharius* have given rise to lengthy discussions. As for the country of origin: the names of the characters, the country in which the action takes place and which the poet seems to know in detail, would lead us to the middle Rhine. The manuscripts bear the name of no author, but some of the better ones contain a prologue in which a certain Geraldus dedicates the poem to a prelate by the name of Erkambaldus.

The adherents of the French origin thesis identify him as Geraldus, monk of Fleury-sur-Loire, but the awkwardness and constrained manner of these few lines contrast so greatly with the tone of the work that they are believed to be the dedication of a scribe and not that of the author. On the other hand, a passage from the *Casus Sancti Galli* would seem to furnish a more solid basis. Ekkehard IV (980-1069) relates that when he was still a schoolboy, his predecessor Ekkehard I (d. 973) had written a "Life of Waltharius Manu Fortis" and that he, Ekkehard IV, had been charged with the revision and correction. Upon closer examination, this version also gives rise to difficulties. It is scarcely possible to see in our *Waltharius,* whose design is clear and whose originality is indisputable, the work of a schoolboy. Indeed, we find there inaccuracies and Germanisms. Where, then, is the revising hand of Ekkehard IV? Moreover, A. Wolf, in the *Studia Neophilologica* of Uppsala (his views are outlined and discussed by K. Strecker[9]) quite recently taking up an observation by Flach, wonders whether we have not been under a misapprehension in believing that the *Vita Waltharii* of which Ekkehard IV speaks, is our poem. A *Vita* is an edifying text and this term would be more suited to a recital of the "moniage" type such as that

[9] *Deutsches Archiv,* IV, 2, 1941.—One can also read with profit: A. L. Corin, *Simples Réflexions d'un curieux à propos des procès du Waltharius et du "Rudlieb";* Musée Belge, XXXIV, 1930, pp. 109-133.

of the Waltharius of the *Chronicle of Novalese*. On the contrary, we can better envisage the singer of the battle exploits
of Walther of Aquitaine writing at a princely court than
in a monastery. We know that Charlemagne had ordered the
collection of the old German songs. The *Waltharius* as we
know it certainly fits better in the ninth than in the tenth
century, and it would thus be the incontestable chef-d'oeuvre
of the Carolingian Renaissance.

In prose, we shall not stop at the theological or didactic
writings whose interest is solely historic. One can still read
with pleasure the *Vita Caroli* of Einhard (770-840). The
Nardulus of the Palace Academy had enjoyed, since 796, the
intimate and trusted friendship of Charlemagne. Then, too,
Fulda where he received his education, owned a manuscript
of the *Lives of the Twelve Caesars* by Suetonius. Einhard
was inspired by the plan of the *Vita Augusti* and took bits
of phrases from it which he applied to his hero. To what
point do the expressions taken from Suetonius conceal reality? Taken altogether, the portrait is apt, and from the literary point of view, holds together admirably. The language
is supple and easy and the borrowed phrases have been incorporated adroitly. In short, it is the best biography which
the early Middle Ages left us. The eighty-odd manuscripts
which have been preserved furnish the most tangible proof
of the success which it won.

We cannot close this chapter without speaking of the correspondence of Lupus of Ferrières.[10] At Fulda, Lupus had
been the pupil of Raban Maur. He was the teacher of Heiric
d'Auxerre. Returning to Ferrières in 836, he became abbot
in 840. "It was by a personal study of ancient and modern

[10] Levillain, *Classiques de l'Histoire de France,* 1927-1935.

authors," says Levillain, "that he made his a humanist's soul." His tastes are revealed in the letters where he is seen in search of manuscripts which could either enrich his library or furnish him with the most correct texts. Elsewhere, he discusses grammar, meter or semantics: but these preoccupations of a scholar and a man of letters go hand in hand with the energy of a leader of men. He dared use the firmest language to the king when it was a matter of the interests of his abbey, and with the sense of reality of the good administrator he did not fear to enter into the most humble details. "Less preoccupied with his role of rhetorician, he contented himself with assuring his means of existence," he wrote to the court during a year of dearth, speaking of himself in the third person.

This evidences a happy equilibrium, and permits envisaging with confidence the future of a Renaissance whose ideal was found to be grafted upon such vigorous personalities. Unfortunately, it was to be put to the test during a very somber period.

The Tenth and the Eleventh Centuries

THE DISINTEGRATION of the Carolingian monarchy led to a decentralization of culture. For a time, the court of Charles the Bald was to reunite poets and men of letters, but the rivalries which weakened the feeble descendants of Charlemagne, the Norman invasions which, from the second half of the ninth century, followed one another almost unceasingly no longer permitted the luxury of the happier years. Already, we have seen, the writers of the second generation of the Caroline Renaissance were connected with the great monasteries of Southern Germany: Saint Gall, Fulda, Reichenau. In the course of the following two centuries the principal centers of culture were to be the monastery schools, and then the cathedral schools. The Norman invasions which annihilated so many centers of study in England and in the West of the continent exerted an influence which was not entirely negative. It was perhaps to escape that threat that Sedulius Scottus came to the Meuse valley. It was the destruction of the abbey of Jumièges (862) which according to legend led one of its monks to Saint-Gall with an antiphonal in which Notker Balbulus (c. 840-912) found the solution to a difficulty which had troubled him for a long time. By what procedure could one succeed in remembering the melody which at the end of the gradual prolonged the *alleluia?* (whence its name *sequentia*). The antiphonal substituted words (*prosa*) for the vocalises. Notker tried to do

[49]

as much with it without obtaining at first a satisfactory result. His teacher, Ison, proposed that he make each syllable correspond to a note. A *sequentia cum prosa* resulted (more commonly called either "sequence" or "prose"). Actually, it is probably not quite so simple, but since the initial *alleluia* and the finals in *"a"* (where the sequence keeps traces of its origin) belong to French pieces, the anecdote probably has some factual basis. This question of the origin of the sequence is one of the most obscure, and there is no general agreement upon the number of authentic pieces by Notker. What is certain is that the new genre was to have considerable vigor. "The Middle Ages," says Father De Ghellinck, (II, 177) "left us more than 5000 compositions of this sort, but of the approximately 150 hymns which the liturgical year had toward 1500, only four were kept in the Roman Missal of Pius V (1572)." The *Stabat Mater* which had no more than the *Dies Irae* been composed as a sequence was added to it in its course. With the *Veni Sancte Spiritus* (beginning of the 13th century) of Pentecost Sunday and with the *Lauda Sion* (in the Feast of the Holy Sacrament) they represent the sequence come to its final evolution. We shall return to this later. The *Victimae Paschali Laudes* by Wipo (d. 1050) which is sung on Easter Sunday is a transition form. There is no regular rhythm, but rhyme already appears side by side with assonance. The following fragments will convey an idea of what the Saint-Gall sequence (which was very close to Notker's) was:

1. *A solis occasu*
   usque ad exortum

2. *est cunctis nomen tuum*   3. *qui inde novum solem*
   deus, laudabile   *mittis mira lege.*

4. *qui lustret orbem radiis*   5. *et foetu terras vegetet.*
6. *hic Columbanus nomine*   7. *dignus habere spiritus*
   columbinae   *sancti pignus*
   vitae fuit.   *in hac vita.*

. . . .

16. *nos ergo tete poscimus*
    beate, quo nos domino
    tu commendas.

The name of Notker also merits recognition as that of a great teacher. At last, today he is identified as the Monk of Saint-Gall, *balbus* and *edentulus,* who between 884 and 887 wrote the *Gesta Karoli* in which we see, says Paul Thomas (*Morceaux Choisis,* p. 45) "how the memory of the great emperor lived in the popular imagination." We are present at the transformation which ushers us from Einhard's portrait to the legendary figure of the Chansons de Geste.

"The tenth century has often been called the age of hagiography: stereotyped and typic." We shall here treat of a genre particularly representative of the medieval spirit and which was remarkably abundant in all the centuries. It would be useless to attempt to enumerate even the most well known of these Lives of the Saints.

For a complete listing, one should refer to the *Bibliotheca Hagiographica Latina* (two volumes and a supplement) of the Bollandist Fathers; for an overview, to the substantial reports given by De Ghellinck.[1] Here we must limit ourselves to a description of what in the *Vitae* belongs to literature: partly by reason of stylistic embellishment: some are

[1] *Littérature Latine au Moyen Age,* Vol. I, pp. 62-67; 161-169; Vol. II, pp. 146-156.—*Essor de la Littérature Latine au XII* Siècle, Vol. II, pp. 164-198.

in verse, (we know that the Middle Ages made little distinction between a work written in poetry or in prose . . . the former were simply "better dressed"), some are in rhymed prose. Some were revised and retouched (because their style seemed old and their Latin barbaric) to suit the taste of the day. These revisions frequently injured the documentary value of the texts. Beyond considerations of their style, the Lives of the Saints belong to literature because they obey certain conventions which are characteristic of the genre. It is easily explained: most of the saints of whom a biography was wanted for divers reasons (the edification of the faithful or the desire to create popular enthusiasm were far from being the only ones) were little known. Perhaps they had lived in distant centuries or countries, or perhaps their lives had not been filled with outstanding events, or perhaps they owed their existence to a misunderstood sentence[2]: in any case, to fill in the gaps of the authentic given facts, the authors fell back upon the resources of rhetoric. A type-plot furnished the canvas upon which it sufficed to embroider the origins, birth, childhood, education, virtues, martyrdom, discovery, translation of the body, and the miracles with which the Saint favored the spot of his tomb. If they run short of inspiration, the hagiographers did not hestitate to insert a certain episode from another *Vita* into theirs. Let us not condemn them! They responded with what was expected of them, and they as well as their public lived in an atmosphere of perpetual miracle. Finally, hagiography, as does the novel today, lent itself to all developments. Using the resources of imaginative literature (not a very fitting

[2] See E. Faral, *Saint Amphiballus* in Melanges P. Thomas, p. 248.

name, actually, for rather than imagining they borrowed themes of proven value) they dramatized the lives of their heroes by means of romantic episodes or marvelous fables. Rather irreverently A. Van Gennep has spoken of "paper-backed novels." One could dwell at length upon this subject. The fine book of the Rev. Father Delehaye, *Les Légendes Hagiographiques* (3rd ed., Brussels, 1927) treats it with the amplitude it deserves. We shall give but one example: the miracle of the ring of St. Arnulf, placed at a later date in the primitive text of the *Vita S. Arnulfi*,[3] is an evident reminiscence of the famous tale of the ring of Polycrates.

In its turn, hagiography nourished other literary genres. Such is the case with the works of Hrotsvitha, the nun of Gandersheim (Brunswick) which date about 965. Ch. Magnin's study and translation (into French) of her dramas gave them a notoriety they do not entirely deserve. In our day, they no longer appear as the almost miraculous products of culture in the midst of barbarism. Their appearance has been understood since it was discovered in what manner classical literary tradition was maintained and since we have realized that the true idea of tragedy and of comedy had been, so to speak, completely effaced.

Terence was certainly read, since it was with the object of warding off the danger which his plays presented that the Saxon nun wrote hers. For the sinful attraction of a dialogue between lovers she wanted to substitute the example of the

[3] Cf. Em. Dony, *L'Auteur Unique des Vies des Saints Amat, Romaric, Adelphe et Arnulf*. Liége 1888.—Also L. Van der Essen, *Etude Critique et Littéraire sur les Vitae des Saints Merovingiens de l'Ancienne Belgique*. Louvain 1907.

chastity of virgins and of the mortification of hermits. The
grotesque was not excluded from these edifying dramas.
Dulcitius is the recital of the misadventures of a governor
who persecuted the Christians. He locks into the washhouse
three young Christian girls whose favors he hopes to obtain. At night he goes to claim them, and clasps in his arms
cauldrons and boilers. He rushes out covered with soot. At
the sight of him the soldiers flee, the doorkeeper wants to
put him out and his wife believes him mad. The three young
Christians are to die in agony for the ridiculous role they
have made their persecutor play. The elder two mount the
funeral pyre, but their souls rise to heaven before the flames
even touch their garments. Angels mock the executioners of
the youngest, and at the moment when she falls, pierced with
arrows, she proclaims that death to her is only another victory. Elsewhere, the conflict is no longer between Christianity and paganism, but between the spirit and the flesh.
Thus we see the hermit Paphnutius lead Thais to repentance
and penitence.

These plays were not destined for staging. Their dialogue
is too rapid for declamatory performance and stage move-
ments. The action is too precipitate and slows down only in
sections which didacticism makes no less incompatible with
scenic necessities. In *Paphnutius,* for example, the reader is
present at an actual lesson, with questions and answers, on
musical theory. Let us note in closing that Hrotsvitha, in her
dramas and in their prefaces, employed rhymed prose.

From the point of view of the theater, the "dramas" of
Hrotsvitha contributed nothing. The drama, nevertheless,
was going to be born again—but from another source; and
the Middle Ages saw history repeat itself in the birth of

tragedy which in ancient Greece had detached itself from a religious hymn.

The sequence and especially the trope often offered alternating choruses, with questions and responses. By a natural development the dramatic dialogue was born while the liturgical pomp was going to develop into a scenic background. The tropes which complete or comment upon a liturgical text (such as the *Introit,* the *Kyrie* or the *Gloria*) disappeared completely at the time of the revision of the Roman Missal. They seem to have been of French origin. Saint-Gall which claims their invention, offers examples only from the 13th century, while the Troper of St. Martial in Limoges is of the middle of the 10th century. We borrow from it the trope composed for Easter which is already in dialogue-form:

1. *Quem quaeritis in sepulchro*
   O christicolae

2. *Jesum Nazareum Crucifixum*
   O coelicolae.

3. *Non est hic;*
   Surrexit sicut praedixerat.
   ite, nuntiate
   quia surrexit.

4. *Alleluia, resurrexit dominus,*
   hodie resurrexit leo fortis,
   filius dei.
   Deo gratias, dicite, eia.

From this was to come the *Officium Stellae* (for Christmas) of which the so-called Munsterbilsen Gospelbook offers a well-known example,[4] the *Officium Selpulchri,* the *Officium Peregrinorum* (for Easter) which are at the beginnings of the Christian drama.

In poetry, the most interesting works of the 10th century are anonymous. The *Gesta Berengarii,* by an Italian from the North (Verona?) are half-way between history and epic. In Italy, we still find, at least in the last years of the 9th century, poetry in the rhythm of the so-called "song of the soldiers of Modena":

> *O tu qui servas armis ista moenia,*
> *noli dormire, moneo, sed vigila!*

It was probably a clerk of Verona who was the author of the stanzas of a somewhat perverse attraction *O admirabile Veneris idolum* addressed to a young boy who was the object of his affection. The meter (accented dactylic tetrameter) is the same as in those verses which were perhaps sung on the feast of Saints Peter and Paul, but which are generally considered to have been the song intoned by the pilgrims when they came within sight of the Eternal City:

> *O Roma nobilis, orbis et domina,*
> *Cunctarum urbium excellentissima, . . .*

Outside of these two successes, the rhythm was scarcely used. There is no agreement upon the date of the two pieces. Gaselee says they are between 800 and 900; according to Raby, they are 10th century, according to Dreves, end of the 11th or beginning of the 12th century. In any case, the epoch of the full flowering of rhythmic poetry was to build its stanzas on other verse forms.

With the prose writers, the use of rhyme became more

[4] Ed. G. Cohen and K. Young, *Romania* XLIV (1916-1917) pp. 357-372.

general.[5] Rhyme itself developed one tendency to become richer (in the 11th century it was frequently of two syllables) and another tendency towards repetition. In the *Vita S. Gerhardi Broniacensis* (written about 1050) we find sequences of 3, 4, 5, 7 rhymes, and there have even been found cases of more than twenty rhymes (*Tiradenreim*). The schools of Belgium furnished a numerous contingent of writers who used this mode of expression for their annals and their Lives of Saints; those of the Schelde and those of the Maas regions used it equally. Milo and Hucbald of S. Amand on one side and Stephanus of Liége on the other, had from the beginning of the second half of the ninth century opened the way which others such as Folcuin de Lobbes, Heriger, the great scholar Adelman, Theoderich of S. Trond, Sigebert of Gembloux, the authors of the Lives of S. Bavo and S. Vincent Madelgaire, and Philip of Harvengt were to follow, to mention only a few.

That much said, it might be fitting to pause a moment with men who stand out as distinct personalities regardless of the form they used. Rathier (890-974) who is called "of Liége" (from his birthplace), "of Lobbes" (where he was educated and later was abbot) "of Verona" (of which he was bishop) had a stormy career. He owed his unhappy experiences to his impossible disposition. Trained at Lobbes (*vallis scientiae*) he "knew" Latin, and since his entanglements furnished him with the opportunity for libelling his rivals and competitors; since his setbacks led him to self-examination; and since a man of this stature has a long experience with men and things, we are disappointed not to find in his works the morsel which would give us at least an ap-

[5] Cf. Karl Polheim, *Die Lateinische Reimprosa*. Berlin 1925.

proximate idea of the author's personality. His *Praeloquia,* after two books which expose the duties of the Christian of any age and of any condition (knight or doctor, teacher or pupil, man of affairs or beggar), continue with a treatise on the duties of princes. The plan is original, but the development is remarkable as it reveals a profound knowledge of Scripture from which he deduces a moral adapted to each particular case. The *Dialogus confessionalis* is rather a lucid and pitiless examination of conscience than a confession in the modern sense of the term where we would seek above all the authentic mark of "having lived." It is a spiritual disposition which makes us little fitted to render justice to writers who in speaking of their own individual cases always kept the thought of their general application before them.

Muratori, the famous editor of the *Rerum Italicorum Scriptores,* characterised the Lombard Liutprand (920-972) perfectly in speaking of the "historian who, in the century of the sword, rose so high above the general ignorance that in spite of his crude style . . . he is still able to captivate and retain the attention of the reader. He had an alert and penetrating spirit and his recital is of an exceptional vivacity and liberty of tone." "Historian" is given with a reservation: he was too inclined to follow his mood to give an impartial account of events—at least of such events in which he himself had been involved. Nevertheless he is an astonishing writer of memoirs. His *Relatio de Legatione Constantinopolitana* contains precisely the sort of material to which we are so partial today and which the Middles Ages offer us so parsimoniously: details "seen." It little matters to us that the portrait of Nicephorus Phocas is carried to a caricature. He is among those who will never be forgotten. One could risk speaking of a Saint-Simon "before letters", if this talent as a portrait painter had been used somewhere else but on repulsive subjects. He thus avenged himself of the humiliations which he had undergone and he does not forget to transcribe the verse which he had scribbled on the walls of the inhospitable residence assigned to him and his suite. It is in analogous spirit that he wrote his *Antapodosis* which may be translated "Give the devil his due." The events of 886 to 962 in Italy, Germany and Greece present the material of this colorful report. He neglects no opportunity to show his personal malice, notably toward Berengar who had burdened him with a first ambassadorship to Constantinople (949) and whose niggardliness he had to remedy out of his own pocket in order to maintain his position. The two works are stuffed with Greek quotations, followed by transcriptions and Latin translations. In the *Antapodosis,* moreover, the prose is intermingled with verse, whether he introduces a discourse, describes a combat, or whether he grows warm and takes a satirical tone.

To the political relations with Byzantium, we also owe the acquaintance with the *Alexander Romance* of the Pseudo-Callisthenes. The arch-priest Leo of Naples had brought back a copy of it from his ambassadorship there in 942, and made a Latin version. Its success is explained by the need for romanticism which was filled by a book relating the adventures of a legendary hero in a fabulous Orient, and also by the ease of a Latin unhampered by grammar and very close to the common language.

This Latin, in short, is that in which (in the 5th or perhaps in the 6th century) the *Historia Apollonii Regis Tyri* had been written after a Greek model of the Hellenistic period. A manuscript of the University of Ghent contains a fragmentary version in 792 leonine verses, composed in the 10th century, it would seem at Tegernsee. The versifier arbitrarily put the narrative in the form of an eclogue (that is to say, in a dialogue between Saxo and Strabo). The literary value is mediocre, but it is another proof of the persistence of the romanesque tradition.

In the 11th century, we see the influence of the cathedral schools become greater. Gerbert who had the reputation of being the most learned man of his century and who was to become Pope under the name of Sylvester II already had been a scholasticus at Rheims from 970 to 982. We need not speak of his mathematical work, but we cannot remain silent about the quality of his humanism and his merits as a writer. His style is supple and elegant and one might be tempted to call it Ciceronian were it not for an occasional phrase foreign to the classic language which indicates that he was ignorant of any paralyzing obsession with purism. One of his letters shows him insisting to his correspondent that scribes capable of copying ancient texts be recruited, and sending them parchment and money for that purpose.

The names alone of Fulbert of Chartres (pupil of Gerbert) and of Egbert of Liége are sufficient to indicate the character of the movement just mentioned.

With Fulbert (born about 960 in Aquitania, died in 1027), begins the fame of a school which was not to be eclipsed until the 13th century by that of Paris, when philosophy took precedence over the study of authors. The alphabetical poem by Adelman (of Liége) shows at the same time the place that the master had been able to gain for himself in the hearts of his pupils, and the radiation of his teaching. But Fulbert, the great teacher, also seems to have been the author, according to all appearances, of the two famous poems which we find in the Cambridge Songs. The didacticism of the beginning of the first:

Aurea personet lira *clara modul anima*
Simplex corda sit extrema *voce quindenaria, . . .*

gives way, in the third stanza, to a charming description of spring:

Cum telluris vere novo *producuntur germina*
nemorosa circumcirca *frondescunt et brachia,*
flagrat odor quam suavis *florida per gramina. . . .*

The sober touch and the quick rhythm make one forget the banality of the theme. As to the other piece, it relates, with a simplicity full of finesse, the adventures of the little Abbot John, who having wished to live like the angels without working with his hands and without eating is led to a more realistic conception of monastic life by eight days of fast.

Egbert of Liége (b. about 970) had much less breadth of knowledge and appears, beside Fulbert, like a petty schoolmaster. The task was difficult, and Egbert complained of the laziness and rustic manner of his pupils. He had attained or passed his fiftieth year when he composed his *Fecunda Ratis* (that is to say, the heavily-laden ship). The first part, *Prora* (1768 lines) is a collection of proverbs or sayings categorized according to length (one, two, three, four lines and more). The *Puppis* edited after it (and shorter: 605 lines) contains longer narratives borrowed from the Latin fabulists and satirists, from the Bible and the Fathers. The necessity for cramping his thought frequently into one or two lines, his use of words diverted from their sense, and allusions incomprehensible to us often make Egbert's thought obscure and his style unnatural. Nevertheless, he drew his proverbs not only from the ancients and from the Bible, but also from the language of the people, from one side or another of the linguistic frontier. Thus the original title of the *Prora: De Aenigmatibus Rusticanis.* "It is no small merit", says Gaston Paris,[6] "for a schoolman from about the year 1000 to have deigned to pick up the pebbles which his contemporaries disdainfully trod on, and it is no slight merit for his poem to be thus the most ancient and the most pure source from which we may draw, in our turn, the knowledge of a notable part of the folklore of the tenth century." Otherwise, there are only popular sayings and sentences drawn from ancient wisdom in the *Fecunda Ratis.* Egbert also imparts to us personal reflections: the ruggedness of the Ardennes inspires him to a quatrain. In sum, the whole atmosphere of the school is evoked, complete with the grammatical remarks and even the scoldings of the teacher, at the epoch when Liége was at the height of its fame.

The abbatical centers were far from a decline. In the contrary, we witness in Italy the re-establishment of the celebrated abbey of Monte Cassino, the ancient foundation of St. Benedict which was to spread its renown for the next two centuries. The hymns of Alphanus of Salerno (as well as the odes which he composed upon the occasion of the dedication of the basilica rebuilt by Didier) are, for Renan, a "last whisper of antiquity." Raby sees there rather the prolonging of the traditions of the Lombardic schools: tradi-

[6] *Journal des Savants,* 1890, p. 563.

tions which had remained alive in Italy through all the adversities which had come upon the country. The secular masters always continued to teach there. Peter Damiani (1007-1072), one of the great figures of the Church at the time when it undertook a great inner reform, had been trained by and taught in these secular schools, before becoming a recluse and later cardinal bishop of Ostia. His *De die mortis,* which eloquently describes the anguish of the soul called to appear before its judge, has for its counterpart the lightness which sparkles in the *rithmus de gaudio Paradisi,* also in catalectic trochaic tetrameters.

He is also the author of *De Ecclesia Romana ab Antipapa Invasa Luctus* which already heralds the bitter satires of the Goliards.[7] This richly endowed poet was equally a polemist and a theologian of merit. A new paradox: this educated man, schooled in the classical writers, who as prior of Fonte-Avellana had established a library for the monastery, was the same man who, in vehemently passionate passages, proclaimed his contempt for the sages and philosophers of antiquity.

Moreover, he is ironic upon the subject of the monks who in disregard of their spiritual perfection, neglected the rule of St. Benedict to follow the rules of Donat. Only a writer of great talent could allow himself such invectives. We almost hear again the voice of Gregory the Great; but in the

---

[7] The attributing to Peter Damiani of a poem commenting upon the *Canticle of Canticles* (and which one could say was a whisper, like a poem by Maeterlinck) no longer seems to be upheld:

> Quis est hic qui pulsat ad ostium,
> Noctis rumpens somnium?
> Me vocat: "O virginum pulcherrima
> Soror, conjux, gemma splendidissima!
> Cito surgens asperi, dulcissima."

11th century the fate of literature was no longer at stake and these eloquent protestations add only one more contradiction to the complex and tormented figure of Peter Damiani.

To come back to the intellectual centers, the abbey of St. Gall continued in the brilliant light of its fame. Ekkehard, fourth of the name, corrected and edited the Waltharius of Ekkehard I (which, therefore, cannot be the epic poem which we know!) He is especially known as the author of the *Casus Sancti Galli* in which he retraces the history of the good and the bad days of the monastery. Its historical value is mediocre, but Ekkehard IV is an amusing raconteur who knows how to sketch character and who gives us a vivid and colorful chronicle of the life of the monastery. Unforgettable is the picturesque trio Notker Labeo, Ratpert and Tuotilo whose diversity of temperament (according to a rule frequently illustrated by novel and film) only emphasizes their unity of heart and spirit (cf. the episode where we see them inflict a well-merited chastisement on a bad brother who had been spying upon their affairs). And when a Hungarian band invades the monastery, rather than intoning a chorus of lamentations as would any other chronicler in a like case, Ekkehard IV tells us the story of Brother Heribald whom his imperturbable simplicity extricated from the worst difficulties and who greeted the returning monks with the surprising declaration that the barbarians in feasting had shown a generosity toward him quite unlike that of the monastery's cellarer.

In the second half of the century, the Abbey of Bec in Normandy was given renown by Lanfranc of Pavia (1008-1089) and by his disciple Saint Anselm of Aosta (1033-1109) who were to succeed to the archbishopric of Canterbury.

The latter has merited being called "the greatest glory of the Benedictine schools." We need not state here the place he occupies in philosophical and theological speculation. He was, in addition, a true writer, whose qualities appear in a voluminous correspondence. In his works, says de Ghellinck (II, p. 129) "the thinker and the writer always reveal the man." He was one of the creators of medieval prose: of a living prose, no longer based on a model, but rhymed and in rhythm, yet a rhythm which follows the measure of the thought.

Still from another monastery—according to all appearance, it was St. Evre at Toul in Lorraine—came the *Ecbasis Captivi*. It was formerly dated as of the 10th century (about 940), but a more careful consideration of the vocabulary and the historical allusions has led Erdman[8] to date it a century later. Many questions, however, remain unanswered: the author is unknown, the real title (*Ecbasis cuiusdam captivi per tropologiam*) remains enigmatic, the localisation of the work is not absolutely certain, although the geographical allusions would place it in Lorraine, not far from the linguistic frontier. The subject of the poem is the adventure of a calf which escapes from its stable, is met by the wolf and led home by him to await being eaten (*per tropologiam* would indicate that it is an allegory: the calf is the inexperienced monk who upon leaving the cloister is exposed to all the perils of the world). A dog, however, has put the parents of the fugitive on his track and the alerted animals prepare to lay siege to the wolf's lair. At that point the fable of the sick lion is introduced (to whose bedside the animals are

[8] *Deutsches Archiv*, IV, 2, 1941. The last edition of the text is that of Strecker, Hanover 1935.

called to propose a remedy), a subject which we find already in an anonymous poem of the 10th century which is preserved in a manuscript of St. Gall and edited with the works of Paul the Deacon.[9] There, however, the victim of the fox's cunning is the bear and not the wolf. We find the theme again later in the *Ysengrimus,* then in the *Roman de Renard*. After this interlude—an explanation of the race hatred which opposes the wolf to the fox—the action proceeds. The denouement is near. The wolf is killed, the calf is returned to his mother and father. The poem contains 1229 leonine hexameters. The rhyme (monosyllabic most of the time) is found in non-accented syllables: that is, it is there only for the eyes. The textual borrowings from the ancient poets, pagan or Christian, and from Horace in particular, are so numerous that, with some exaggeration, a Cento has been mentioned. On the whole, the work presents little attraction for the reader of today. A mass of allusions which its contemporaries would understand (those at least who lived in the circle for which it was composed) escape us completely. What is clear is that the people who speak and act before us are monks. Whatever the intention of the author, he inaugurated a new genre in Western literature: that of the beast-epic.

The *Ruodlieb,* also an important prototype, dates from the middle of the 11th century. Maurice Wilmotte called it "our first courtly romance"; "our" because in envisaging certain aspects of the vocabulary too exclusively, he believed it to have been written in the "in-between" country, but by a Romanic author. It has been recognized since that it is very hazardous to draw on the argument of so-called Romanisms or Germanisms which are found throughout medieval Latin.

[9] M. G. H., *Poetae Latini Aevi Karolini* I, 62.

Moreover, it is very difficult to localise in Lorraine a work whose autograph manuscript (or at least the fragments which we have) comes from Tegernsee. "Courtly Romance" is only partially exact. The courtly spirit appears only in spots, but the term romance characterizes very well a complex work in which elements of a very diverse nature are mingled.

The following resume will permit the reader to form his own judgment. It is important to note first that it is difficult to determine what part of the whole is represented by the two thousand-odd verses which remain, and second that the connecting of the episodes which the fragments preserve, is more or less conjectural.

Ruodlieb is a knight who has placed his sword in the service of a foreign monarch. Following a war in which he distinguished himself by his valor, he shows his competency in the negotiations and manages an interview (which is described for us at length) between his master and the conquered king. Acceding to the desires of his mother, Ruodlieb is going to return to his native land. He bids farewell to the king who in recompense for his services gives him a choice of his treasures or his store of wisdom. Ruodlieb chooses the latter, and the king then gives him (besides two loaves of bread which he must not cut except in the presence of his mother and which conceal precious jewels) twelve counsels which in the course of his voyage he is led to violate. The fragments give us the recital of the misadventures which follow the transgression of three of the rules. Ruodlieb at last meets one of his nephews who is searching for a fiancee. He accompanies him and both are received at the castle of a noblewoman with whose daughter the young man falls in love. Then comes the recital of Ruodlieb's return to his

mother and the marriage of the two young people. Ruodlieb
in his turn thinks of taking a wife and has fixed his choice
upon a neighboring lady, but having learned that in the
matter of virtue she is not completely irreproachable, he
makes her look upon the proofs of her misconduct. Moreover, a dream has made the mother foresee a more brilliant
union for her son. The last episode shows us Ruodlieb in
conversation with a dwarf whom he has seized at the en-
trance of his cavern and who promises in return for his liberty to show him the place where the kings Immunch and
Hartunch hide their treasures. It will be necessary for him
to fight with them, but if he succeeds in conquering them,
he will be able to wed Heriburg, the daughter of Immunch.

Thus, the last fragment takes us into the legendary world
of the Germanic epic. The narration of the interview of the
two kings must have been inspired by a real event: the meet-
ing of the emperor Henry II and of Robert, king of France
(1023). The ceremony of the court, such as is described in
fragment V, presents a very striking analogy with that which
was in use at the Imperial Court of Byzantium. In contrast,
the story of the twelve rules of wisdom is typically a tale of
oriental origin according to all appearances, although the
realism with which certain episodes are treated makes us
think of the fabliaux. The diversity of sources is no less remarkable than the variety of styles: influence of hagiography,
influence of the romances of the earlier epoch (the scene in
which we see Ruodlieb playing a harp recalls an episode of
the Historia Apollonii Regis). What can one say finally of
those passages in which the author complacently dwells
upon the talents of his hero as a huntsman and fisherman,

and in which he enumerates the variety of fish with an erudition disconcerting to lexicographers?

Despite this complexity, despite also the fragmentary state in which it has come to us, the romance keeps an evident unity of tone. One can recognize everywhere that truly exceptional gratuity in the literature of the time which frees it of all moralizing, satiric or didactic aim. In addition, we find throughout that the author possessed a remarkable experience of the world and of life at a time when most writers could not rid themselves of a bookish and scholarly tone. It also offers an extremely curious picture of the customs of the time. Unfortunately, the gifts of observation and maturity of spirit of the author are hardly well served by his talent as a writer. His Latin is incorrect: plainly he was thinking in German. As to the verse (leonine hexameters), it seems to have been composed as an exercise. Platitude is its most constant characteristic.

The graceful episode in which we see a young couple dance to the sound of a harp does not inspire the author to anything higher than prosaicness. Was he destitute of a sense of its beauty? At least this is only revealed negatively in the piece in which he traces a portrait of the aged woman which foretells that of Villon's "La Belle Heaulmière."

Interesting as are such works as the *Ruodlieb* or the *Ecbasis,* they are overshadowed by a collection compiled in the 11th century, which allows us to form an idea of the taste of the epoch and the importance of poetry. Were the *Cambridge Songs* written in the monastery of Canterbury where we know them to have been from the 12th to the 16th century? The writing denotes an Anglo-Saxon hand, but the pieces in the collection come from the continent. Of the 49 numbers which it contains, it has been established that in whole, numbers 2-15 come from a German archtype; numbers 35-47 are of French origin; number 48 is the *O admirabile Veneris idolum* which we have already met. It is more difficult to assign a precise origin to the other pieces. There are extracts from the ancient poets with neumic notation which indicates that they were intended to be sung. Other pieces in which the vernacular is mixed with Latin lead us again into Germany, to the section of the middle Rhine. The collection seems therefore to have been composed for a lover of that region. Its last editor, Strecker, has shown how much the hypothesis of the repertoire of a vagabond (assuredly a tempting one) had been blown into thin air.

What do we find there? Sequences both religious and profane, which attest to the favor which this new form had attained. There is one on the coronation of the emperor Conrad II; there is the history of Lantfrid and Cobbo, a story of a test of friendship, where conjugal love sacrifices itself for friendship, and the wife is respected by the friend;[10] the story of the snow child (*Modus Liebinc*),[11] the praise of Otto the Great (*Modus Ottinc*); the *planctus* on the death of the emperor Henry II; a "chanson de menterie," theme found in many a popular tale; and also a piece of pure scholarly character on the Pythagorean theory of musical tones. In the second part we note an alphabetical poem of Merovingian origin on the theme of the fragility of things human. Its presence is astonishing in our collection. Then there is the

[10] See the story of *Amis et Amiles* which Raoul of Tourtier (below, p. 77) will tell in his Epistola II (Ad Bernardum).

[11] A subject which we will encounter again in the *De Mercatore*, a Latin fabliau edited in *La "Comédie" Latine au XII*e *Siècle* (see below, p. 98).

naive story of the she-ass of the Homburg convent which
was eaten by the wicked wolf; the tale of Heriger, archbishop of Mainz, who confounds and severely chastises the
false prophet who claims to have gone to Hell and then to
Heaven. The verses, divided into hemistichs of five inter-
rhyming syllables, are in an easy Latin of free rhythm.

We understand that in the last century, when romanticism
was in full swing, the savants spoke of "popular poetry."
The misunderstanding was scarcely possible, however, with
number ten by Fulbert of Chartres: a panegyric of the nightingale, a theme already treated by Eugen of Toledo (middle
of the 7th century) and by Alcuin. Nor was it possible to
misunderstand No. 23 where the *Natureingang* follows its
course with the evocation of the songs of different birds.
The theme goes back to a fragment of Suetonius (*de naturis
animantium*) in which the nomenclature of the verbs designates the cries of animals and of which the grammarians
naturally made use. The *Anthologia Latina* has preserved
such verses. Their clearest merit is that they are mnemotech-
nic. Our poet, at least, has drawn from this lexicographical
treasure with discretion.

It is remarkable that this already erudite art, in spite of
some awkwardness, renews an old theme and gives us the
illusion of a direct contact with nature. In another piece
(*Iam dulcis amica venito*) the influence of Ovid is combined
with that of the Canticle of Canticles, but there are common-
places in it to which a true poet can always give an air of
novelty.

Several stanzas have been inked over by censorship in the
Cambridge manuscript; but other manuscripts, two of which
are from the tenth century, fortunately help us to restore

them. The *Versus Eporedienses,* elegiac distichs added towards the end of the eleventh century, to a Psalter of Ivrea, develop more at length the theme of the *Invitatio Amicae* (found again in the pastoral) and introduce into it a new motif, the *descriptio formae pulchritudinis.*

Still more "modern" are the *Verna Feminae Suspiria* in which the beauty of springtime oppresses the heart of a young girl and makes her burst into sobs. Manifestly, we are in the presence of something unheard of: out of the breaking up of ancient verse, out of the pedantism of scholarly imitations has come a new poetry which we feel sometimes in one or the other piece, but of which the Cambridge manuscript really offers us the first fruits.

In the schools, however, the rules of classic prosody were studied and applied with some license. Hexameter and the elegiac distich were sometimes adapted to the taste of the day, and leonine rhyme was the most usual form. Towards 1100 they were used by men of the first order: Hildebert of Lavardin (or of Mans, of which he was bishop), 1050-1133; Marbod of Rennes (1035-1123); and Baudry of Bourgueil (1046-1130). The first two are the best known, at least by reputation, because, in the 18th century, they found an editor in the person of the Maurist Beaugendre whose work has been reprinted with some additions in the Patrologia (Vol. 171). The work of B. Hauréau (*Les Mélanges Poétiques de Hildebert de Lavardin*) and quite recently that of Dom A. Wilmart (*Revue Bénédictine,* XLVIII, 1936) have justified certain hazardous attributions. It was known that the *Floridus Aspectus* must be left to Peter Riga, the *Vita Mahumeti* (ed. Huebner, *Hist. Vierteljahrsschrift,* Vol. 29,

1934) to Embrico of Mainz. Dom Wilmart, in restoring the collection which had been uncritically reprinted by former editors, has sorted out from the *Miscellanea* (P. L. 171, 1381-1442) and from the two Supplements (ibid., 1279-1282; 1447-1458) the work of Hildebert. The latter comes out reduced, but not diminished. The authorship of the most important pieces is confirmed and they prove an incontestable talent, but the perfection of the rhetoric is of a sort to which modern readers are not susceptible. The Elegy on Rome is the work of a great poet. When Hildebert went to the eternal city, the soldiers of Henry IV, the Saracens and the Normans of Robert Guiscard had just accomplished its ruin, and the spectacle of desolation inspired in him verses so beautiful that they were included in anthologies of classic Latin poetry when their author was unknown. No less noble in sentiment is the reply in which Hildebert makes Christian Rome speak.

Rather than poetry, it is eloquence, but eloquence served by a peerless aptitude to use contrasts and to balance antitheses. We must cite also, among the most famous pieces attributed to Hildebert, the *De Excidio Trojae* (*Pergama flere volo*)[12] and the poem on his exile—for his career as a bishop was turbulent—where, with his habitual virtuosity, he treats the commonplace theme of the inconsistency of fortune. Upon occasion, he also varies the rhythmic verse with equal ease. His hymn to the Trinity (*Alpha et Omega, magne Deus*) is counted among the masterpieces of mystic poetry.

[12] The attribution has been contested. On the popularity of the subject of the Trojan War see A. Boutémy, *Le Poème* Pergama flere volo . . . *et ses Imitateurs du XIIe Siècle. Latomus* V (1946), pp. 233-244.

Let us recall in passing Hildebert's prose writings: his letters which promptly became famous and which were used as models in schools; and his sermons. Beaugendre had collected forty-one, but a close study of the manuscript tradition led Dom Wilmart (*Revue Bénédictine* XLVII, 1935) to reduce this number to nine. These are still fine days for the criticism of attribution!

Like Hildebert who was educated at the cathedral school of Mans and was a teacher there later, Marbod (c. 1035-1123) was at first a pupil at the cathedral school of Angers, his native town. Baudry of Bourgeuil was his schoolfellow. He was a scholasticus there before being called to the episcopal seat of Rennes. A result of his teaching there is the treatise *De Ornamentis Verborum,* which consists of briefly formulated rules, each followed by an example in verse. It is the first in date of those Arts of Poetry which occur in increasing numbers towards the end of the 12th and the beginning of the 13th centuries. We would hear more of the rest of his work, if his talent were not on so many counts so similar to that of Hildebert. The impersonality of that poetry explains the confusion which the collections of Hildebert have suffered with those of Marbod and which modern critics have tried to clear up. A title, an allusion, the careful comparison of different manuscripts help to restore each to his own right. Of the style which belongs to a great poet in his own right and by which we recognize him among a hundred others, they scarcely speak. Is it too subjective a criterion? No doubt, especially as the personal accent was a thing too rare in the Middle Ages to be taken into account.

The most important work of Marbod is his *Liber decem*

Capitulorum into which an autobiographical section is introduced; even there, however, it is difficult to make a distinction
between what has been lived and what is mere scholarly
amplification. His best known work is his *Liber Lapidum* or
Liber de Gemmis which was as much in vogue as the
Physiologus. The Physiologus of which prose versions exist
from the high Middle Ages, was put in verse, together with
an allegorical interpretation for each of the twelve animals
by a certain Magister Theobald, an Italian, it seems, of the
11th or 12th century. Just as the *Physiologus* was the original
of the *Bestiaries,* the *Liber Lapidum* was to originate several
Lapidaries in the vulgar tongue.

The recent edition (by P. Abrahams, Paris 1926) of the
whole of the poetic work of Baudry, Benedictine abbot of
Bourgeuil (later archbishop of Dol) reveals to us a rather
strange figure of a man of letters who placed literature first
among his preoccupations and for whom all circumstances
(a letter to a friend who is tardy in writing, a remonstrance,
condolences) offered an occasion to versify short pieces—
pieces whose brevity did not save them from being monotonous. He was the victim of his too fluent talent in a society
which furnished him with too many occasions to show it.
There were specially the "Rolls of the Dead" (rotuli) which
the churches and the abbeys sent around to announce the
death of a bishop, an abbot, even a monk, to recommend
him to the prayers of the sister-communities. At each stop,
the roll was lengthened by several lines of condolences. The
virtues of the defunct were recalled, an intercession was asked
for him. How could Baudry have escaped from this pious
duty?

Longer pieces permitted him to apply the full measure of his talent; such as the *Pseudo-Ovidiana:* a letter from Florus to Ovid with the answer of the exiled poet; two Heroides, *Paris Helenae* and *Helena Paridi,* in hexameters which exclude all intention of plagiarism. Neither is there parody in the sense in which we understand it today. His classic erudition shows again in a long moralized mythology. The poem addressed to the Countess Adele, daughter of William the Conqueror, has given rise to numerous studies because in describing the decoration of the Countess' chamber (a theme frequently treated by the ancients, and which conveniently introduced narrative or didactic excursions) Baudry depicts a tapestry upon which are embroidered the episodes of the conquest of England. Was that the famous Bayeux Tapestry? The man of letters reveals himself in notes to his scribe and to his illuminator, and in verses which he consecrates to his notebooks or to a broken stylus (*De graphio fracto gravis dolor: quippe stilum tantae condere molis erat!*) Nothing indicates that it was meant ironically. Ovid had not taught him to smile! The whole man we find in the *De Sufficientia Votorum Suorum* where he describes the kind of life which would have pleased him, had he been free to choose: the bourgeois ideal of Plantin's Sonnet is expressed with the aid of reminiscences from Tibullus.

Baudry was perhaps not a true poet save in one piece: a *planctus* upon the death of Hubert of Meung, his former master. "The refinement of consonances, the change of rhythm and refrain" caused E. Du Meril to insert it in his famous collection of *Poésies Populaires Latines Antérieures au Douzième Siècle* (1843) although it belongs to metric poetry.

To the Hildebert-Marbod-Baudry[13] group we must now add Raoul of Tourtier (Radulfus Tortarius, about 1065-1120), monk of the celebrated abbey of Fleury-sur-Loire. Fleury, Angers, Le Mans: it was toward the West 'of France and toward the country of the Loire that the centers of literary activity, which were formerly situated in the territory of the Rhine and in Lorraine, were moving.

A *Passio S. Mauri* and some *Miracula S. Benedicti* did not differ from contemporary hagiographic production. The recent publication (by Marbury B. Ogle and Dorothy M. Schullian, *American Academy in Rome* 1933) of the whole of the poetic work of Raoul makes us see in him a representative of that scholarly humanism which marvels at antiquity and demands examples from it. The *De Memorabilibus* is but a versified edition of the work of Valerius Maximus; the eleven epistles, however, are personal. Their elegiac distichs are, it is true, monotonous and his verse never reaches the dignity which a Hildebert and a Marbod were able to give it. But questions of form aside, to judge by the variety and interest of subjects treated, he retained something of the teachings of Horace.

[13] They are the best known because their works are easily accessible, but they are perhaps not the best nor the most interesting. Too many pieces are scattered in various publications, or still unedited, to permit a definite judgment. On this, see the suggestive remarks of M. A. Boutemy, *Autour de Godefroid de Reims,* in *Latomus* VI, 1947, pp. 231-255.

The Twelfth Century

THE TWELFTH CENTURY was the great century of medieval Latin letters. First, it was the one in which the new form of poetry which was its most original contribution to the intellectual patrimony of the West, came to its complete development. The new form had appeared in the last centuries of the Empire, when the feeling for the quantity of syllables had been lost. It then showed itself in vigorous works at the time when the Carolingian Renaissance, while restoring classical studies, held the poets in a rut of completely artificial versification. The development of the sequence in the 10th century, and the Cambridge collection in the 11th century, definitely proved the vitality of the new form. It has been called "popular poetry"; a rather unfortunate term, since Latin was now the language only of the clerks, but it is rather apt if one understands the phrase to mean that the poetry was adapted to the new level of Latin used by the men of school and Church. This was no doubt a limited circle, but it was very active and exercised almost a monopoly over the arts. The term "rhythmic" or accented poetry (although Nicolau, A.L.M.A.IX, 1934, p. 55, makes a distinction between the two terms) is closer to reality. The idea of quantity had disappeared, but that of accent was very much in evidence. We know that in words of two syllables, the emphasis is on the first. In those of more than two syllables it is on the penultimate if it is long, on the antepenultimate if it is not. Then, since it is natural for the human voice to mingle tonics and atonics (or stressed and unstressed syllables) there arises around the accented syllable an alternation of the weak and strong syllables affected by a secondary accent; and in a verse form based on accent they are made similar to those which have the principal accent. Naturally, therefore, there is established a binary rhythm (the ternary rhythm based on the dactyle or the anapest, is much rarer) which is either ascendant or iambic ($\smile \acute{\smile}$) or descendant or trochaic ($\acute{\smile} \smile$). It must be noted that these terms borrowed from metric poetry are used here only by analogy. The schema: 7 — $\smile$ applies not to a line composed of seven trochees, but a line of seven *syllables* in trochaic rhythm. (*ut hóminés salváret*). The line is actually based on the number of syllables; a number which must be the same for corresponding lines.

The rhyme whose use extended also to metric poetry (the leonine rhyme especially, affecting the two hemistichs of the same line; but there are many other combinations), soon became a characteristic of accented poetry. At first it was optional, later employed only in couplets, then extended to all the lines in a stanza with the most varied combinations: rhymes solely masculine (iambic or ascendent rhyme); solely feminine (trochaic or descendent); interlaced rhymes, etc. Their rhyme scheme is shown with letters. Thus, the following stanza:

> *Ecce mundus demundatur*
> *totus enim uacuatur*
> *mundus a mundicia*
> *Nichil habet mundi mundus*
> *cum in sola sit fecundus*
> *uiciorum copia.*
>
> (WALTER OF CHÂTILLON)

is represented by the following scheme:

$$2 \times 8 - \smallsmile a + 7 \smallsmile - b$$
$$2 \times 8 - \smallsmile c + 7 \smallsmile - b$$

We should note that with the poets of the Middle Ages rhyme did not always correspond to the modern definition: homophony of the two accented syllables. They were sometimes satisfied with an identical vowel or final consonant in the last syllable, or even with assonance. It was not until the twelfth century that one could see the use of rhyme in two syllables made general; but the *Scoti* had been forerunners in that path. It is, however, impossible in the present state of our knowledge to establish a very strict chronology which the discovery of unknown texts might not upset.

The influences which provoked or at least favored the development of rhythmic poetry have always been a much debated question. Wilhelm Meyer of Speyer, the great expert on the subject, has studied the influence of Byzantine hymnology (*Gesammelte Abhandlungen zur Mittellateinischen Rhythmik*). P. S. Allen (*The Romanesque Lyric,* p. 200) defends the hypothesis of Arabian influence, either direct or indirect, through the intermediary of the Goths of the province of Septimania "the remnant of the Gaulish dominions of the Visigothic Kings"; but he also admits the influence of Irish poetry. Numerous *Scoti* had traversed the continent, and their predilection for rhymed and rhythmic verse is known. It seems more logical, nevertheless, to seek in the Latin itself the internal factors which brought about that revolution in the technique of poetry. We have said that it was favored by the fact that the sense of quantity was completely lost (cf. the soldiers' songs, especially that one transmitted by Vopiscus, *Vita Aureliani,* 6). Mathieu Nicolau[1] emphasizes the influence of the Roman schools in Africa of the 5th and 6th centuries, where at the same time the art-prose combining isokola and homeoteleutes developed, in addition to the technique of verse which "realized the harmony of the ictus and the unrestrained accent, and to obtain this result observed the coincidence of the feet (trochees) and the words." The catalectic trochaic tetrameters composed by Fulgentius in 533:

Thespiades Hippocrene | quas spumanti gurgite. . . .

would be the oldest example of accented versification.

The complete disappearance of rhythmic verse was manifest in religious poetry where the sequence was subjected to the strictest rules. A regular rhythm and general use of the two-syllable rhyme characterize the so-called Victorine style —for it is in the graduals of St. Victor that this type was most perfectly represented and appeared in the greatest variety of forms. The Breton Adam (of whom we know almost nothing except that he entered the regular canonry of the abbey of St. Victor near Paris in 1130[2] and that he died there toward the end of the century) is the uncontested master of that kind of poetry. However, as happens in such cases, pieces not written by him were attributed to him, such as for example the famous prose of the nativity of Mary:

Salve mater salvatoris
Vas electum, vas honoris
Vas celestis gratiae.

[1] *Les Deux Sources de la Versification Latine Accentuelle,* A.L.M.A., IX, 1934, pp. 55-87.
[2] Which became famous, at the same time, through the mystical theology of Hugo and of Robert of St. Victor.

which borrows from the Canticle of Canticles its most passionate accents to celebrate the Virgin-Mother.

The complete cycle of the liturgical year furnished Adam with the subjects of his proses, but had he been inspired by Marian devotion only, he would have found a variety of resources in allegorical literature, so highly valued in the Middle Ages—a variety such as pages of quotations could not sufficiently describe. We should also mention here a number of anonymous pieces, or pieces whose traditional attribution is now contested. Their chronology is therefore uncertain, and so much the more since less developed forms continued to be cultivated by the very contemporaries of the Victorines. Even St. Hildegarde, the great visionary of Bingen (1098-1179), has left us some sequences and hymns which are in truth sketches in prose, probably dictated to a secretary in the fire of inspiration, pieces of a passionate intensity.

At Pentecost, the Church still sings the sequence *Veni Sancte Spiritus* formerly attributed to the French king, Robert the Pious, or the German monk Herman Contractus and with more credibility to Pope Innocent III or to the archbishop of Canterbury, Stephen Langton.

No less famous, the *Iesu Dulci Memoria* as it figures in the Office of the feast of the Sacred Name of Jesus is taken from a long poem whose author was not St. Bernard (more probably an English Cistercian) but "in which we find condensed in rigourously precise formula all the teachings of the abbot of Citeaux." "It is also," says E. Gilson (*Les Idées et les Lettres,* p. 39 ff.), "one of the most moving expressions of medieval piety."

Let us mention also, somewhat at random, the hymns of

Reginald of Canterbury, a native of Poitou who died in the first years of the century; and those of Osbert of Clare, prior of Westminster; and those of Guido of Bazoches (died 1203).

But the greatest name is that of Abelard (died 1142) who was not only the dialectician and the master who assembled attentive crowds around him at the foot of Mont Ste. Geneviève, or in more distant retreats, but the author of the *De Calamitatibus Suis,* an autobiographical narrative in which he retraces the history of the passion which united his name forever to that of Heloise. His love had inspired him with verses which all Paris sang (*Me plateae omnes, me domus singulae resonabant,* wrote Heloise) and which we have probably lost. Later he was to use his talent to compose hymns and complaints (the latter were not destined for liturgical use) for the house of Paraclete of which Heloise was the prioress. They occupy a place for themselves in hymnology. The rhyme is poor, the meters varied and Abelard invented new forms of strophes; but in this field he remained alone and did not form a school.

The infinite variety of resources of the rhythmic strophe are better revealed in pieces of secular inspiration. Amourous poetry, pastoral, satire, complaint, parody: all these genres having found an adequate means of expression had a sudden but brief flowering at the same time. If their diversity offered the poet the most varied possibilities, it also authorized a liberty of form which was naturally forbidden to religious pieces which were often intended to be part of the Office.

It would be an error, however, to imagine that there existed a barrier between religious and profane lyric. There were, of course, on the one hand the monks such as an Adam of St. Victor who composed their proses in the peace of the cloister, and on the other hand we picture the wandering scholars singing bawdy couplets or bawling drinking songs. Often, though, it was the same man who composed light poems and who celebrated the glory of the Virgin Mary. This is not altogether incompatible: they were great sinners who found extremely touching accents to speak their repentence and to bare their souls.

One of those was Walter of Lille (where he was born about 1135) or of Châtillon (where he taught). It has been established (this is not without interest) that he explained the *auctores* in the entire texts, and not in the florilegia, to his pupils. He was in the chancelry of Henry II of England which placed him in contact with the circle of humanists around John of Salisbury. We will find him at Bologna, studying canon law, and at Rome. The satiric pieces directed against the Roman Curia were dictated by personal experience.

In the manuscript of St. Omer (K. Strecker, *Die Lieder Walters von Châtillon,* 1925) we find hymns celebrating the mystery of the Incarnation or the miracles of St. Nicholas side by side with pieces of very free inspiration, such as the idyll whose heroine is Glycera and the ending of which is scarcely left in doubt by the implications of the last stanza. These were sins of youth. Comes the age of forty, the age of reflection. "I have served the flesh too often," he said "and now that I believe that all which is flesh is destined for death, I want to serve the Creator." And when the sickness came upon him (it is said that he was stricken by leprosy), he sends a moving prayer to the Redeemer (*Dum Galterus egrotaret*) and while he does not say "I," the tone is most personal. It is a rare thing and therefore we note it in passing.

Yet it was in satire that Walter found the opportunity to display his gifts. His witticisms about the vices of the Roman court were inexhaustible.

In the famous *Propter Sion non tacebo, sed ruinas Romae flebo,* he utilized the allegory of the perils of the sea not to represent the temptations of this world, as did Adam of St. Victor, but to represent the grasping prelates of the Curia. Charybdis and Scylla are a constant menace for the imprudent one who would venture in these parts, and if he is not swallowed up, the sirens prepare themselves to seduce him:

> *Dulci cantu blandiuntur*
> *ut Sirenes et loquuntur*
> *primo quedam dulcia:*
> *"Frare, ben je te cognosco,*
> *certe nichil a te posco*
> *nam tu es de Francia.*

Two words of half-French, half-Italian jargon (what an apparent informality in this erudite poetry!) evoke the honeyed smile which welcomes the stranger, but malicious observation soon gives way to the most virulent invective.

The Feast of Fools offered to the lower orders of the clergy an opportunity for self-expression in all freedom for a few hours. They denied themselves nothing, naturally, especially when a Walter lent his talent to the occasion. The extraordinary virtuosity with which he rails at prelates and dignitaries of the Church is evident in the long piece which Dom Wilmart found in a manuscript of Charleville[3] and which groups in 53 goliardic stanzas of one source most of those which

[3] Cf. *Revue Bénédictine,* XLIX, 1937, pp. 322 ff.

K. Strecker had collected from fourteen manuscripts:[4] mytho-logical or scriptural allusions, stanzas with *auctoritas*,[5] al-literations, plays upon words; he uses all the resources of his art with an unheard of wit and the reader never tires of this prodigious hocus-pocus.

The recent studies of Dom Wilmart have restored to Walter the *Sermo Goliae ad Praelatos* which was formerly published under the name of Walter Map, together with other pieces among which is the famous *Apocalypse of Golias* (of probably English origin). The *Utar contra vitia carmine rebelli* which figures in the *Carmina Burana* and which has sometimes been attributed to the Archpoet is probably not by Walter, but, according to Strecker, must have come from his school. These questions of attribution are often difficult. We can not always trust the indications of the manuscripts. Many works remain anonymous, and many great personalities lived in a sort of legend which had grown around their names. Such was the case with Hugo of Orleans, the mysterious Primas, until the day when W. Meyer of Speyer published a series of pieces taken from an Oxford manuscript which allow us to judge his talent and which have established his biography accurately. He was born in 1095 and one poem can be dated 1144 to 1145. His occasional poems make him appear, says Madame Dobiache-Rojdes-

---

[4] Nos. 4-7 of his *Moralisch-Satirische Gedichte Walters von Châtillon*. Heidelberg 1929.

[5] That is to say those whose last line is a quotation, generally taken from a classic poet. For example:

Roma datis opibus   in tumorem crescit
et, quo plus infuderis   magis intumescit;
nam sicut Oracii   versus innotescit,
    sincerum nisi vas, quodcumque infundis, acescit.

vensky,[6] almost like a personification of the general idea of Golias, the mythical eponym of the Goliards: "an irascible, proud, temperamental parasite . . . an indefatigable insultor of the closefisted Maecenas, or of anyone who won money from him in gambling, of women who deceived or scorned him, him of the ugly face and the short stature. . . . In the celebrated piece *Dives eram et dilectus* (which was also to enrich the collection which goes under the name of Walter Map) he contrasts bitterly his brilliant youth, happy and carefree, to his miserable decline."

It is the rather unhappy tale of poets whose formidable satiric genius condemned them to lasting hatreds. Walter of Châtillon and the Archpoet had this unhappy experience, and later Villon, "the last of the Goliards and the greatest of them all."

The real personality behind the pseudonym of the Archpoet is still unknown. All that we know is that he was a protegee of Rainald of Dassel, the arch-chancellor of the emperor Frederick Barbarossa and archbishop of Cologne. This places his poetic activity about 1160.

The Confession of Golias (*Estuans intrinsecus ira vehementi*) would be enough to ensure his fame. The confessions of Walter of Châtillon and of the Primas were those of sinners trembling at the thought of having to appear before God. The confession of the Archpoet is the defense plea of a client who has fallen into disgrace. Never were the ideals of these poets (*Wine, Women and Song* is the title of the book dedicated to them by J. A. Symonds) expressed with greater or more cynical candour nor in more striking lines:

[6] *Les Poésies des Goliards,* Paris 1931, p. 39.

Meum est propositum in taberna mori,
ut sint vina proxima morientis ori . . .

Philip de Grève (1180?-1236), chancellor of the church of Paris, is well known for his conflicts with the Dominicans and with the University. A moralist who combined fragments of Horace and words of the Scripture, he lifted his voice to upbraid the simoniacal cardinals in the *Bulla Fulminante*. However, this bitter satirist could find the most simple and touching words to sing the song of Mary Magdalene and he succeeded in clothing with effects of infinite tenderness the stark antithesis:

> 2. *Iesum quaerens convivarum*
> *turbas non erubuit*
> *pedes unxit, lacrimarum*
> *fluvio quos abluit,*
> *crine tersit et culparum*
> *lavacrum promeruit.*

> 3. *Suum lavit mundatorem,*
> *rivo fons immaduit,*
> *pium fudit fons liquorum*
> *et in ipsum refluit,*
> *caelum terrae dedit rorem,*
> *terra caelum compluit.*

This diversity of ideas and forms, and even the circumstances of the life of Philip de Grève (one could say as much for a Serlo of Wilton) show us once more with what care and discrimination the terms "vagants" and "goliards" (which we were once very tempted to apply to all the authors of satiric or critical pieces) must be used. Otto Schumann, in the preface to the new edition of the *Carmina Burana,* describes the vagant as "the independent writer, the author who lived by his pen thanks to the protection of rich patrons." He reserves the name "goliards" for the wandering clerks. Only in rare cases can we identify the poetry of the vagants with love lyric. The love poems, almost in their entirety, are anonymous,—no wonder, considering the frequently liberal tone of certain pieces. They are of a great variety, and the whole of this small book could scarcely give an outline of the subject. We will have to confine ourselves to the broadest generalities. Some of the poems show an artful technique, others affect an evident simplicity. Bits of verse in the common language were inserted here and there. Let us not forget that it was a "poetry of society, made not only to be enjoyed, but to be sung in company . . . most of the goliardic pieces can only be understood if we consider the *concio scolaris* in the background which is, at the same time, audience, actors and chorus."[7] The vocalises (et a et o; eia, eia . . .) which were interpolated like a refrain into so many poems (and where some scholars wanted to see an influence of folksong) were in themselves, no doubt, a way of letting the whole company take part in a song whose words they did not understand.

A tableau of spring sometimes provides the theme of the whole poem. More often it serves only as an introduction (*Natureingang*) to an idyl. April, the burgeoning grass, the woods clothed in their new finery, the song of the nightingale: the charm of these pictures must not blind us to their banality; and if perhaps some less common descriptions (*Mane garrit alaudula | lupilulat et cornicula* . . .) makes us

[7] O. Dobiache-Rojdesvensky, *Les Poésies des Goliards*, p. 69.

imagine a poet "lending a brotherly hand to a winged world," the philologist, alas, reminds us that these variations are the work not of an "intimate friend of the forest," but rather those of a schoolboy devoting himself, as so many others (cf. *Carmina Cantabrigiensia*) to an exercise for which the lexicographers would furnish him with material. It matters little, however; for the cheerfulness of the air makes us forget its banality and the artificiality of its words. If this transmutation has taken place, it is because a poet has been at work.

The idyl is sometimes chaste (*Ludo cum Caecilia*) but what follows shows us that this was an exception. Moreover, the courtly conception of love was completely foreign to the goliards. Sometimes the heroine is a shepherdess, and our Latin texts offer the prototypes of a genre which was going to have a lasting popularity under many different forms.[8]

Sometimes it happens that the shepherdess makes the advances. Generally she resists, less (it is true) in solicitude for her virtue than in fear of being beaten.

The lack of feeling which characterizes these songs at least assures them of a negative quality: the absence of all sentimentality. And when the adventure turns into drama, the frankness with which the seduced and abandoned girl recounts her lamentable story moves us more than the most tearful complaints.

We cannot leave love poetry without saying a word about *Phyllis and Flora,* (an anonymous piece, Italian or more probably French of the first half of the 12th century) and

[8] See M. Delbouille, Les Origines de la Pastourelle, *Mémoires de l'Académie Royale de Belgique,* Cl. des Lettres, 2ᵉ série, vol. XX, 1926.

about the *Council of Remiremont* (c. 1170). These are the prototypes of the *"Debate of the Clerk and the Knight."* The discussion of their respective merits in love has been begun by Phyllis and Flora in a lovely spring scene. Eventually, the argument is submitted to the Cytherian goddess. The mythological erudition and the influence of Ovid indicate clearly that the author is a learned clerk. We can guess in whose favor he will arbitrate the conflict. The discussion of the nuns of Remiremont comes to the same conclusion, but this time in a scandalous atmosphere of parody. Let us note in passing how much the debate was in favor in the course of the Middle Ages. *De rosa liliique certamine* (by Sedulius Scotus), *Conflictus ovis et lini* (by Winric of Trier) *Pulicis et Musce Jurgia* (by William of Blois)[9] *Altercatio fortunae et philosophiae; de Clarevallensibus et Cluniacensibus; Conflictus aquae et vini, vini et cerevisiae,* etc., show how the rivalries of nationalities, social classes and religious orders furnished material for developments whose tradition was tied up with the dialogues of Virgilian shepherds (cf. *Ecloga Theoduli*).

The scholarly circle from which our clerks came also explains their preference for parody. Laughter at the expense of their masters and what they taught was a revenge which the schoolboys naturally took for the boredom of lessons and the severe punishments reserved for the lazy.

Our parody "in the manner of" which is a purely literary diversion, scarcely prepares us for a just appreciation of the parodying wit of the vagants. They were content with some similarities of phraseology or rhythm. The atmosphere of

[9] Discovered and published by M. A. Boutémy (*Latomus* VI, 1947), pp. 133-146.

the tavern or the joy of speaking their mind to the mighty does the rest. We juxtapose here two stanzas of a hymn to the Virgin (11th century) and of a drinking song which came from it:

1. *Verbum bonum et suave*
   Personemus, illud ave
   per quod Christi fit conclave
   Virgo, mater, filia.
6. *Supplicamus, nos emenda,*
   Emendatos, nos commenda
   Tuo nato ad habenda
   Sempiterna gratia.

1. *Vinum bonum et suave*
   Bibit abbas cum priore
   Et conventus de peiore
   Bibit cum tristitia.
5. *Supplicamus, hic abunda*
   Omnis turba sit facunda
   Ut cum voce nos iucunda
   Personemus gaudia.

In the same way, grammatical terminology was to provide material either for more or less broad allusions or satires on the Roman Curia and the Pope:

> *Nam qui fore debuit gratie "dativus"*
> *factus est ecclesiae rerum "ablativus"* . . .

Our poets had a predilection for vague approximations:

> *Romam avaritiae vitet manus parca,*
> *parcit danti munera, parco non est parca,*
> *nummus est pro numine et pro Marco marca,*
> *est minus celebris ara quam sit archa*

says the 12th stanza of the famous *Utar contra vitia*. We note the play on words upon which were grafted the numerous *Evangelia secundum Marcas Argenti*. The malice of some of these pieces made them worthy of being reprinted by Flacius Illyricus in his *Varia Doctorum Piorumque Virorum De Corrupto Ecclesiae Statu Poemata* (Basle 1557) which thus became the first printed collection of Goliardic poems. It was to attribute to them an exaggerated importance to see in them forerunners of the Reformation! They were frequently nothing but exercises and, moreover, the most violent attacks upon the Papacy were directed against its abuses, not against the institution itself.

The triumph of rhythmic verse must not be interpreted as an eclipse of traditional poetry. The latter, on the contrary, was more abundant than ever and became more varied. A master of the rhythmic strophe such as Walter of Châtillon was equally as good as versifier of the hexameters of the *Alexandreid* for which the romantic history of Quintus Curtius furnished him with the essentials. Its success was lasting, and in spite of the change in taste, three editions came out in the course of the 16th century.

The crusades had given birth to narrative poems; sometimes in hexameters, like Fulco's (first half of the 12th century) and sometimes in elegiac distichs, like the poem by Guilo of Toucy (died c. 1142).

Towards the middle of the century, Bernard Silvestris, one of the masters to whom the school of Chartres owed its glory, composed the *De Mundi Universitate* in which verse alternates with prose. Here, under the influence of Neo-Platonic thought (which comes in more or less directly through the Pseudo-Dionysius, John Scotus Erigena and Macrobius' commentary on the *Dream of Scipio*) he "has represented the active principles of the Creation in the form of personified beings" and "brilliantly described the great labour of nature working under the supreme authority of God."[10]

[10] E. Faral, *Revue des Deux Mondes,* September 1926, p. 449.

The same conceptions are found with a pupil of Bernard, Alan of Lille; first in the *Anticlaudianus* (a reply to the theory of St. Hilary of Poitiers quoted by Claudianus Mamertus) and then in the *Planctus Naturae,* a composition of mixed prose and verse like the *De Consolatione* of Boethius. Allegory plays a large part in it, as well as in the *Architrenius* by John de Hanville, composed in part under the influence of the *Planctus Naturae.* An analysis of these works, too long to give here, can be found in the above mentioned article in which Faral studies the sources of the ideology of the *Roman de la Rose.* Here too, the French writers of the 13th century only take up again and continue the Latin literature of the 12th century. With Alan of Lille and John of Hanville the tendency was from the metaphysical to the satiric, passing through the didactic. Moral preoccupations once again, dominated by mysticism (but which manifested themselves also in the bitter satire of the vices of this world) dictated the well known verses of the *De Contemptu Mundi* to a monk, Bernard, whom we must be content in calling "of Cluny." (Saint Bernard being quite out of question and all proposed interpretations for the adjective *Morlanensis* being subject to caution). He admirably expresses in it the aspirations of the soul which pines for the celestial Jerusalem. We know only too well his invectives against woman which the monastic literature of the proverbs and exempla used as a constant source of inspiration, repeating them endlessly. At the end of the Middle Ages, we find a proliferation of them on the margins and fly-leaves of manuscripts, as *probationes pennae.* We note the particular structure of his hexameter (already practiced by Hildebert), the tripartite division emphasized by the interior rhymes and the final rhyme.

The procedure at length produces monotony, but gives vigorous scansion to the sentences.

Under the same title and upon a somewhat analogous theme, Serlo of Wilton told (in elegiac distichs) the vanity of the things of this world, with more conviction than he had in his youth when he had cynically avowed his weaknesses in verses such as:

> *Pronus erat Veneri Naso, sed ego mage pronus;*
> *pronus erat Gallus, sed mage pronus ego.*

His conversion was sincere: after having been a teacher in a Parisian school, he became a Cluniac monk at first and then, looking for a stricter rule, he became a Cistercian monk. He finally became abbot of Aumone. With Nigel Wireker, precentor of Christchurch at Canterbury, satire took a narrative form. His *Speculum Stultorum* is the recital, in elegiac distichs, of the tribulations of the ass Burnellus. Discontent with the tail which the Creator had given him, he goes to consult Galienus in Salerno hoping that the brilliant doctor will have a remedy. Burnellus is the unsatisfied monk who aspires to glory and honors, and the different countries through which he travels furnish Nigel with the opportunity to attack Parisian students, monastic orders (the Cistercians in particular), secular canons, bishops, kings, and as always, the Roman Curia.

Another satire whose plot had a quite different fortune, is the *Ysengrimus* (1148) by Nivard, a monk of Saint-Pierre-au-Mont-Blandin in Ghent. It was, in fact, the source of different versions of the *Roman du Renart* whose prodigious diffusion we know, but which even lately was believed to

have come "from the people and not from books." The re-
searches of Lucien Foulet have made us reverse the formula,
and the animal fable is only one subject among twenty where
the study of the literature of the clerks (that is of Latin expression) has reversed the wild hypotheses on the subject
of the origin of literary genres. It is not necessary to detail
the contents of the *Ysengrimus:* we find there the characters
and a number of the episodes which were to make the *Roman
du Renart* popular: how Renard succeeds in stealing a ham
from a serf and how the wolf eats it (this is the only stroke
of luck for the pitiful hero who gives his name to Nivard's
work), how Renard happens to catch the cock and how
the latter succeeds in escaping from the teeth of his assailant.
The sick lion and the assembly of the animals, introduced
into the *Ecbasis Captivi* as a separate tale, is here but one episode among many others. Another well known episode is
that in which Renard, having stolen a curate's rooster, is
chased by the parishioners. Each one arms himself with
whatever he can find: candlesticks, staves of processional
crucifixes, books. . . . Renard leds the howling pack of pur-
suers toward the place where he has left his comrade, whose
tail is caught in the ice of a fishpond. The poor Ysengrim is
perishing under the blows, when the curate's maid comes
along armed with an axe. The first blow misses; in confusion, she invokes Saint Excelsis, Saint Osanna, Sainte Brigitte,
Sainte Pharailde and Saint Celebrant, and Nivard does not
overlook giving us a sample of how she mangles the Latin
of the Mass: *Oratus fratrus, Paz vobas.* All this is pleasant,
but slows the action. What would it have been if the author
himself had not felt it necessary to abridge the invocation

of these real and imaginary saints? It is only in line 115 that the decisive blow which cuts Ysengrim's tail falls and permits him to flee in pitiful condition.

The name "elegiac comedy" is scarcely a fortunate one, aside from presenting a peculiar association of words. Elegiac simply signifies that the piece is written in distichs formed by a hexameter and a pentameter. Comedy, on the other hand, according to the theorists of the Middle Ages, by no means implied a work of dramatic character. The term was applied to writings on comic or familiar subjects in which the characters were not from the higher ranks of society. There have been attempts to find a more apt title. Faral proposed "Latin Fabliau" (*Romania*, L, 1924); Gustave Cohen who directed the edition of the Corpus of these pieces (in two volumes, Paris 1931) called it the *"Comédie" Latine en France au XIIe Siècle,* using cautious quotation marks. This collection which now permits us an easy comparison of texts formerly very scattered, shows very precisely that their only common characteristic is that they are in elegiac distichs (still, the *De Nuncio Sagaci* is in leonine hexameters!).

Otherwise, they are extremely disparate. Their length varies from 22 to 792 lines (most, however, have from 300 to 550) and only a few are bare of all narrative element. The *Babio* alone, however, possesses a true dramatic character. Some are derived from the ancient theater: the *Geta* is none other than the classic *Amphitryon,* but probably Vitalis of Blois knew it only through the intermediary of an imitation of an earlier time. The *Aulularia* or *Querolus* by Vitalis of Blois also relates not to the play by Plautus, but to an anonymous *Aulularia* of the 5th century. William of Blois states that he took the *Alda* from a Latin adaptation of Menander's

Androgyne. Actually, he had stayed in Sicily, where traditions elsewhere forgotten might have been extant—but nothing definite is known about that.

The other pieces owe nothing to ancient comedy but their titles (*Miles Gloriosus*) or the names of certain characters. There is too little to speak of any influence. On the other hand, Ovid's influence is very clear. He never ceased being read and imitated in the Middle Ages and the *Art of Love* taught our authors the art of painting passion in meticulous but conventional fashion and describing the maneuvers of lovers and the tricks of the go-betweens (cf. *De Nuncio Sagaci, Baucis et Thraso, De tribus Puellis*). In contrast, the title Fabliau marvelously fits the *Milo* by Matthew of Vendôme which was a fable of oriental origin; the *Miles Gloriosus,* a story of the good fortune of a handsome cavalier who tricks his bourgeois associate and manages to escape the snares which a suspicious husband lays for him; the *Lydia,* by the same author as the *Miles Gloriosus,* a subject later taken up by Boccaccio and which furnished the most licentious episode of one of Lafontaine's Fables; and other briefer pieces which are only broad farces.

The works which escaped anonymity (Vitalis and William of Blois, Matthew of Vendôme), came from the Loire region. Evreux and Lisieux are alluded to in *Pamphilus, Glisceria et Birria.* According to the origin of the manuscripts, it would be necessary to assign an English origin to *Baucis et Thraso,* and to *Babio.* It is fitting to pause a moment with this last piece. The character which gives it its title, a stingy and cowardly greybeard, pretentious and stupid, assures the unity of a double plot. At first we see him paying attentions to his stepdaughter; but he is supplanted in the girl's heart by the young cavalier Croceus. He resigns himself, therefore, to remaining faithful to his wife, Petula; but upon learning that he has been tricked by Fodius, his valet, he wishes to punish the guilty ones and is taken in his own trap. After two pitiful failures he decides to become a monk.

The movement which carries the action along, the vivacity of the dialogue, a constant awareness of the scenic necessities make it a perfectly stageable play (which does not mean that it was ever staged!) We note also that several scenes are found again in *Pathelin,* in Ben Jonson's *Volpone,* as well as in the *Etourdi* and the *Fourberies de Scapin.*

The other pieces in the collection, however, hesitate between tale and scenic dialogue. They did not succeed, either, in finding an equilibrium between a humor (whose coarseness alone would have sufficed to hinder the development of a theatrical art) and a pompous style which was as incompatible with the exigencies of the tale as with those of dramatic action. In the bargain, the affectation of such a piece (without any intent on the author's part to make us smile) reaches buffoonery: "His face can hardly hide his anger under a faint smile. The passion which moves him is hard put not to break out openly. His anger is prepared to open the lock of his thoughts with the key of his words; but with the finger on the latch, the ruse prevents the lock from opening." (*Miles Gloriosus* I, 237-240).

All in all, with the exception of *Babio,* these are hybrid pieces, full of awkwardness, faults of taste, good situations poorly exploited, and strongly marked with the imprint of the school atmosphere in which they were born. The comic element in certain descriptions or certain portraits becomes evident when we see the standards of the Artes Poeticae for the description of the beauty of a woman or a palace applied to the description of a masterpiece of pastry or the repulsive ugliness of Geta or Spurius. Amphitryon is no longer a captain coming back from a victorious campaign, but a bachelor who has been studying at Athens. Geta, not content with carrying his master's books, has wanted to retain their contents, and when he meets his double, he gropes in the dark, doubting his very existence, and tries to reassure himself by philosophical reasoning. We must always be careful not to read into the monologue of Geta or the one in which Babio expresses astonishment at living without his vital principle, a criticism of the abuses of scholastic logic. We are only in the 12th century, and this criticism is still a long time away.

We cannot conclude this review of metric poetry without mentioning a category of didactic works of rather mediocre literary merit, but which are no less important for the understanding of the aesthetics of their time than Boileau's *Art Poétique* is for the 17th century.[11]

The *Artes Poeticae of the 12th and 13th century* edited or analysed by Faral[12] are those of Matthew of Vendôme (author of the *Milo*) (c. 1175); of the Englishman Geoffrey of Vinsauf (beginning of the 13th century); of Evrard the German (middle of the 13th century); of Gervasius of Melkley (beginning of the 13th century) and of John of Garland (about 1180-1252).

The *Ars Poetica* of Horace was a "letter of literary direction" in which the friend of the Pisos treats unsystematically diverse questions relative to the profession of the writer.

[11] How much they contributed to integrate in modern thought the topics of ancient literature has been demonstrated by Ernst Robert Curtius, *Europaeische Literatur und Lateinisches Mittelalter*, Berne 1948.
[12] *Bibliothèque de l'Ecole des Hautes Etudes*, No. 238, 1923.

Boileau's *Art Poétique* is an exposé of a doctrine. The Poetical
Arts of the Middle Ages are rather collections of precepts
and models. The precepts go back especially to Cicero (*De
Inventione*), to the *Rhetorica ad Herennium,* and to the *Ars
Poetica* of Horace. These were either misunderstood (amplification, which was the art of showing the validity of an
idea, became the method of developing a subject), or they
were applied so rigidly that Horace's remarks on possible
character treatment became strict rules which, in application, could lead only to conventional figures. "The men of
the Middle Ages lost sight of the individual in considering
only the categories in which the individual entered" (Faral,
p. 79). Further, there is the distinction between the three
kinds of style: the simple (*humilis*), the temperate (*medio-
cris*) and the sublime (*gravis*) as formulated in the *Rhetorica ad Herennium,* which was a means of distinction between the qualities of persons. The "Wheel of Virgil" was
to schematize this theory which left to shepherds the names
of Tityrus and Melibeus, the staff, the sheep, the meadows
and the beech trees; to peasants the names Triptolemus and
Codrus, the plough, cattle, fields and apple trees; while the
names Hector or Ajax had to be given to chiefs of war who
alone held claim to the sword and to noble animals such as
the horse, and who would discourse of cities and camps and
would be sheltered by cedars and laurels. What a temptation for parody in this code of literary propriety!

In contrast, the plays on words which writers only allow
on the stage now and which they leave to lovers of puns were
an ornament of the highest style in the Middle Ages. The
reader will have noticed the few citations which we have
made of examples of these juxtapositions of words of near-

consonance, or of the same word in different forms: *parco-parca, Marco-marca, nummus -numine*. This was the *annominatio*. It was not the exclusive property of parody or light poetry:

> *curant non aras, sed haras; non vera, sed aera;*
> *non aequum, sed equos; non inopes, sed opes.*
>
> (PETER RIGA, *Aurora*)

Trained in this practice, the versifier learned (if one may use the expression) to suck out words and to extract from them all their substance. The following lines give an example of the *determinatio* (which consisted of juxtaposing grammatical groups similarly constituted, each of which amplified a word, just as a schoolboy develops each division of his theme with brackets:

> *surgimus; egredimur; Joachim non excipit hortus,*
> *floridus ut recreet taedia nostra locus.*
> *Nostro blanditur locus arridetque labori.*
> *ridentem reddunt quatuor ista locum.*
> *Haec sunt: arbor, humus et fons et avis; viret arbor,*
> *vernat humus, garrit fons, cytharizat avis.*
> *Arbor fronde viret, pubescit gramine tellus,*
> *murmure frons garrit, gutture ludit avis.*
> *Flos oculos pascit, nardus nares, avis aures;*
> *Hic placet, haec redolet, exprimit illa melos.*
>
> (PETER RIGA, *Versus de Sancta Suzanna,*
> P.L. 171, 1281.)

Finally, to show better the symmetrical value of the grammatical groups, they were placed in parallel columns (vertically). This tour de force is evidently possible only for short pieces:

Natus	Casta	Nitens	Exsultans	Perfidus	Emptus
rex	virgo	sidus	angelus	hostis	homo
quaerit	nescit	dat	declarat	perdit	adorat
nos;	labem;	lumen;	gaudia;	iura;	Deum.

(PETER RIGA, *Floridus Aspectus,* ibid. 1390).[13]

This verbalism, this exploitation of all the possibilities offered by a word is the outcome of an implicit aesthetic which E. Anitchkof studied (*Le Moyen Age,* 2nd series, Vol. XX, 1918, pp. 3-40). It did not seek harmony of line and beauty of images (a purely carnal hedonism and unworthy of man) but demanded a certain activity on the part of the reader. We allow poetry to take a word from its function as an ideogram to restore to it its primitive property of evocation. The writers of the Middle Ages, on the contrary, exerted themselves to reveal the complete idea picture which the word carries within itself. From this came the species of gloss which was the *determinatio,* and in a certain manner, the *annominatio.* Its aim was not to make words clash for the pleasure of hearing their jingle, but it seemed that in making them clash it could shake all they meant out of them. This was the origin of these symbolic and richly associative commentaries:

Littera gesta docet, quid credas allegoria
Moralis quid agas, quid speres anagogia.

Alan of Lille expressed, in admirable lines, the idea that

[13] Cf. the diversions of our fantastic poets:
"*L'acier, l'eau, l'éléphant, l'oignon, l'oeil, la verdure,*
Perce, coule, barrit, se plume, voit, ne dure.
(TRISTAN DERÈME)

nature is only the mirror of our fate. The rose which is for us color and perfume, is according to that conception a symbol and a lesson:

Omnis mundi creatura   *Nostrum statum pingit rosa*
quasi liber et pictura   *nostri status decens glosa,*
nobis est et speculum;   *nostrae vitae lectio:*
nostrae vitae, nostrae mortis,   *quae dum primo mane floret,*
nostri status, nostrae sortis   *defloratus flos effloret*
  fidele signaculum.   *vespertino senio.*

Ergo spirans flos expirat,
in pallorem dum delirat,
  oriendo moriens.
simul vetus et novella
simul senex et puella
  rosa marcet oriens.

(MIGNE, P.L., 210, 579)

We understand also that, in a text, less attention was paid to the expression than to the idea which it held. Where we are shocked by the immodesty of the words:

alvus tumescit virginis
partu dei et hominis,
virgo circumdat virum. . . .

(WALTER OF CHÂTILLON)

the medieval man saw only the dogma of the Incarnation. Here again we could easily multiply the examples, but it will be enough to borrow one from the plastic arts: that of the "Virgo paritura" which gave a concrete expression of the words of the *Salve Mater Salvatoris:* "Mary, most noble receptacle of the Trinity."

What the Poetic Arts were to poetry, the *Dictamina* or *Artes Dictandi* were to prose, but less instructive because they were intended only for letter writing. The oldest treatise on the subject which has come to us is the *Breviarium de Dictamine* of Alberic of Monte Cassino (second half of the 11th century) to whom we must also, without doubt, assign the regeneration of the *cursus* in the documents of the Papal Chancellery. But this takes us away from literature properly so called. In Italy, the *Ars Dictaminis* was above all taught at Bologna, famous for its teaching of law. In France, it was the glory of Orléans, as was the study of poets the glory of Chartres. These tracts joined practice to theory. Models composed either for the occasion or borrowed from the letters of certain famous writers applied to the most varied cases the composition in five parts: *salutatio, captatio benevolentiae, narratio, petitio, conclusio.* They were sometimes merely pure literary exercises: letters from Ulysses to Penelope, complaints of Job to Fate (is the time so distant when the schoolboys would have to compose the "letter of Francis I to Charles V after the battle of Pavia"?). It also happens that they plunge us into a reality so homely, so living that, were it not for the Latin, such a letter from a student to his parents (the *petitio,* naturally, was a request for funds) would seem to be of today.

The prose writers of the 12th century were so numerous that we must resign ourselves to describing only a few. ,

A Saint Bernard (1090-1153) whose strong personality filled all of the first half of the century, goes infinitely beyond the frame of literary history. It is curious, however, to see how even he submitted to the tyranny of the literary modes of the time. In his homilies, his main procedure of exposition is just an analysis of the words of the text in which etymology plays the principal role. "Saint Bernard," says Vacandard, "never came across a proper noun without demanding its inner secret."

He was a mystic, not a savant, and this turn of his spirit left its imprint on the Cistercian libraries which have been conserved. The Scriptures, the writings of the Fathers and liturgical works dominate in these libraries. Theology is sometimes represented there, as well as some secular authors, but there is almost nothing of law, medicine or philosophy. The business of the *scriptoria* was, before all else, to furnish the choir with liturgical texts. Illumination and ornamentation of manuscripts was proscribed. In another field, the Cistercian churches, without bell-tower or sculptures, are still witnesses of his indignation at the fantastic fauna of the tympanums and the Roman capitals. In his youth, he had had a very great liking for poetry and his style is imbued with biblical reminiscences to such a point that we can extend his own expression *"Ruminatio Psalmorum"* to include all of the Scripture. However, he scarcely read the Church Fathers, and he distrusted secular writers. Where he is not sustained by biblical quotations, his qualities as a writer are most clearly revealed. He could not write without passion, but this did not exclude a very fine sense of observation. In his *Tractatus de Gradibus Humilitatis et Superbiae* (before 1125), an account of his conversations with the monks of Citeaux on the Rule of St. Benedict, he paints portraits which would not (says Vacandard) demean the gallery of La Bruyère's *Charactères*.

But it is perhaps in his letters that the personality of St. Bernard appeared at its best. His rebukes are compressed in short sentences in which antithesis is substituted for reasoning. He overwhelms his correspondent with questions and drives him into capitulation. He is there completely, with his inflexible will, with that "common sense in exaltation" which is found in the great mystics,[14] and with his fierce tenderness.

To Saint Bernard, who professed to disdain letters and who figures in the history of literature in spite of himself, John of Salisbury (c. 1110-1180) forms the greatest contrast. A disciple of Bernard of Chartres (he explains at length in his *Metalogicon* what was the method of this great teacher: *exundantissimus modernis temporibus fons litterarum in Galliam*), he also followed Abelard's lessons. He was secretary to Thomas Becket, succeeded in escaping after the latter's assassination (1170), and completed his career in the archiepiscopal seat of Chartres. He is the author of the *Polycraticus sive de Nugis Curialium et Vestigiis Philosophorum,* a political treatise, accompanied (as the sub-title indicates) by numerous digressions. In the *Metalogicon,* he examines the state of logic and philosophy. He is certainly not their adversary, but he presents a vigorous defense of grammar—that is, of the study of letters—, as of the indispensable basis without which philosophy soon turns into a vain disputation about words. In the school of the new Cornificius, they discussed whether the pig led to market was held by the man or by the rope. What came from this school? Improvised philosophers, arrogant monks in their cloisters, doctors who after a trip to Montpelier or Salerno, saw in their art only a method of exploiting their clientele. We note another poem: *Entheticus de Dogmate Philoso-*

---

[14] See Daniel Rops, *Mystiques de France.* Paris 1941.

phorum, and the Lives of St. Anselm and St. Thomas of Canterbury. His work reveals him to us as a true humanist: his knowledge of Latin classics (if he did not know certain authors, he seems to have known others of whom we have lost all trace); the quality of his supple and delicately shaded prose which was admirably wed to the movement of his thought (doubtless the best which was written in the Middle Ages); and especially the optimism with which he affirmed his confidence in the formative value of belles-lettres.

The prologue of the *Polycraticus* sounds like the famous plea which Cicero, defending an obscure poet, pronounced for the defense of literature. Does it not also foreshadow Thomas More and the Christian humanists for whom the doctrine of the Gospel was the flowering of all the good which ancient wisdom contained?

How remote is the joyous conviction of the profession of faith (*Polycraticus* VII, 11), where he expresses his double ideal of philosophy: *veritas et charitas,* from the discouraging pessimism which proclaimed the vanity of human knowledge! His humanism, however, was still incomplete, since he contented himself with asking only lessons of wisdom from antiquity. In Horace and in Juvenal whom he quotes as *Ethici* he saw moralists. Lucan was for him especially the historian, and under the disguise of fables Virgil expressed philosophic truths. The *Aeneid* recounts in allegorical form the history of human life from infancy to old age (*Polycraticus* VIII, 24). But why stop at these deficiencies in the presence of a lucid and well-balanced thought and an author who formed his own individuality from reading the ancients? Let us realize that antiquity for his contemporaries—the first version of the *Mirabilia Urbis Romae* dates from 1150—was still a stage of marvels, before which they stood like great children, openmouthed with stupefaction and admiration!

A little later, William of Malmesbury (c. 1095-1143), who may be called the first English historian worthy of the name since Bede, wrote the *De Gestis Pontificorum Anglorum* and the *De Gestis Rerum Anglorum*. In the latter he inserted the then widespread legend of the discovery of the Treasures of Octavian. Gerbert who, like Virgil, enjoyed the reputation of being a magician on account of his knowledge, succeeded in penetrating to the secret treasure cave. He finds himself in the presence of golden and bronze statues which come to life as soon as anyone tries to lay his hands on the displayed treasures. His servant who thought he could outwit their vigilance, finds all the statues stand up at once and an archer of bronze let fly his arrow, striking the candle which lights the cavern. The two men owe their safety only to a precipitate flight. Such were the fables which fascinated the imagination then. The courtly romances were to take a great part of their marvels from them.[15]

Another source of the marvelous, or rather the source of the whole cycle of "Romans Bretons" was the famous work of the Welsh monk, Geoffrey of Monmouth, apparently a contemporary of William of Malmesbury. His *Historia Regum Britanniae* gave a new life to the Arthurian legend whose tradition previous to 1135 had been scattered and inconsistent. The new elements with which Geoffrey enriched it were taken, he tells us, from a *vetustissimus liber Britannici sermonis*. This assertion has given rise to lively discussions.

[15] See Faral, *Recherches sur les Sources Latines des Contes et des Romans Courtois*. Paris 1913.

The last two editors of the Historia defend diametrically opposite theses. For Faral, Geoffrey is a clever writer, endowed with a singular talent for utilizing and adapting for his own use the reminiscences of his wide reading, but he does not merit to any degree the confidence of the historian, and the *vetustissimus liber* plainly was a figment of his imagination. For Acton Griscom, on the contrary, the examination of Welsh "Bruts"—even on the basis of the few which have been published (and in unsatisfactory editions)— shows that, far from being translations of the *Historia,* they represent an independent tradition to which the *vetustissimus liber* would also belong. The systematic study of Welsh manuscripts has unfortunately only begun. Whatever will be the outcome of the controversy, one fact has been ascertained: the immediate success of Geoffrey's work and its appendages (*Vita Merlini*). Wace was to find in it the material for his *Brute,* and Chrestien de Troyes the material for his Arthurian Romances.

A renewal of interest for the Celtic traditions manifested itself also at the court of Henry II, king of England (1154-1189), in a less romantic but more solid manner. Gerald de Barri (Giraldus Cambrensis, 1147-1223) is the author of the *Topographia Hibernica,* the *Expugnatio Hiberniae,* and the *Itinerarium Cambriae.* His *Gemma Ecclesiastica,* written for his Welsh clergy, is significant as a testimony to the ignorance which was, alas, not the monopoly of the lower clergy.

Welsh folklore also occasionally enters the *De Nugis Curialium* of Walter Map (1140-c. 1209), the writer who, through the poems which were attributed to him, appeared as a typical Goliardic character. He was, in fact, a great personality. After having studied in Paris, as so many others, he entered the royal household when Thomas Becket was still chancellor. His *De Nugis Curialium* (the name recalls the subtitle of the *Polycraticus*) is one of those miscellaneous works which defy all attempts at classification. We find there fables, tales, jokes, anecdotes of diverse origin. The tone is frequently satiric and biting. The court circles which he knew well are not spared, but he was particularly hard toward the Cistercians.

While these essayists give us an idea of the diversity of things which occupied the interests of an elite whose highest aspirations were represented in John of Salisbury,[16] other works, on a decidedly lower level, met with a success which shows that they satisfied the taste and mentality of a large public.

We will only mention the *Historia Caroli Magni* which goes under the name of the archbishop Turpin (ed. Meredith-Jones, Paris 1937). The legend of the great emperor is mixed with that of the valiant Roland. About the connections of this text and the famous Chanson de Geste numerous books have been written. In contrast to Bedier, Meredith-Jones thinks that the romance of the Pseudo-Turpin was originally independent of the *Liber Calixtinus* of St. James of Compostella which was compiled for purposes of publicity and which contains a very curious "Pilgrims' Guide." (Ed. G. Vielliard, Macon 1938).

The *Disciplina Clericalis* was written at the beginning of the century by a converted Spanish Jew, Petrus Alfonsi. He

[16] We must mention here also the Letters of Peter of Blois (about 1135— after 1204) which are nourished with many reminiscences of classical Latin and which owe much to the *Polycraticus;* also the *Otia Imperialia,* a miscellany of history, geography and folklore, composed by Gervasius of Tilbury for the entertainment of the emperor Otto IV.

himself explains in his prologue the plan and purpose of his work which was to instruct the clergy. He took his materials from Arab proverbs and moral tales, from narratives, poems and animal fables. Thus, by way of Spain, the tales borrowed from the treasure of Oriental narrative literature penetrated into Western Europe. They are set in the frame of a story: an old man, feeling his end near, gives advice, in form of fables, to his son. The Latin of these tales, easy and very close to the common language, probably contributed as much as their intrinsic value to the assurance of their success. In these tales in which the characters are sketched more than summarily (the king, the philosopher, the peasant, the old man), a crafty wisdom triumphs over the most troublesome situations, and that so much more easily because all of it happens in a world as free of the slavery of reality as that of our modern animated cartoons. Typed like this, they offer no vantage point to the corrosive influence of time. The reader of today will recognize in a dialogue between a master and the servant who comes to tell him of the death of his dog the story of *Tout va très bien, Madame la Marquise* which we do not sing any longer, but which was so popular about 1936. (See also Jacques de Vitry, *Exempla,* Ed. Crane, CCV)

In 1184, John, monk of Haute-Seille (*de Alta Silva*) dedicated to the bishop of Metz (the oldest manuscript comes from Orval) his *De Rege et Septem Sapientibus,* better known under the title of *Dolopathos,* from the name of one of its principal characters. Although he had little studied the rules of Priscian and had hardly lingered over Quintilian and Cicero, he nevertheless wanted to record, he said, an authentic history which he probably had from oral tradition. In fact, what he recounts is a story of Indian origin, but in which Virgil *"de Manthua, Siciliae civitate oriundus"* takes the place of the sage Sinbad. The king Dolopathos entrusts to him his son Licinius. Upon returning to his country the latter is accused of such an odious crime that he is going to be burned on the stake. The seven sages then intervene; but their fables (among which we find the story of the treasure of king Rhampsinites and that of the pound of flesh given as a bond) only succeed in obtaining a reprieve for the young prince. The intervention of Virgil, riding a huge bird, leads to the discovery of the true culprits who receive their punishment. The story continues with the arrival of a disciple of Christ who answers all the questions which Licinius asks him and finally leads him to baptism, along with a great number of his people.

The anonymous *Historia Septem Sapientium* represents a rather different version of oriental stories of the same family. Here the action takes place in India. This version, quite awkwardly translated from the Hebrew, seems to have come from Jewish centers in France, either in the 12th or in the 13th century.

The End of the Middle Ages

EVEN AS the French seventeenth century actually did not end until 1715, the twelfth century, with Stephen Langton, Walter Map, Philip de Grève, was prolonged until about 1225. But the century of the cathedrals and of scholasticism was, in the domain of Latin letters, almost a period of decadence. It was yet a relative decadence; but divers factors were soon to make it absolute: the substitution of the *artes* for the *auctores;* that is, of theories for the direct contact with the texts. The constitution (1208-1209) of the University of Paris, on the other hand, established the supremacy of the schools where philosophy was taught. The prestige of these studies (John of Salisbury had a presentiment of it in his *Metalogicon*) was fatal to the teaching of letters. Finally a public for literature in the vernacular came into being, while the Latin writings became limited to the clerks, and their character became increasingly bookish and scholarly. The living literature was from then on that of the laity; and translation into Latin appeared as a sign of success. (In Belgium, for example, Jean Bukelaaere translated the three *Martijns* of Jacob van Maerlant, and a certain Baldwinus dedicated to Jean de Dampierre a verse translation of the Flemish *Reynart*).

While formerly the living springs of Latin literature were carried over into the vernacular, the movement now was reversed. Naturally, Latin continued for a long time to be the language of technical and scientific works. It was not really a paradox that Dante wrote in Latin the *De Vulgari Eloquio,* a defense and illustration of Italian as a literary language. He certainly recognized the value of a "dead" language: that it is beyond the influence of time, place and customs. It is the object of grammar to define its laws: *hinc moti sunt inventores grammaticae facultatis; quae quidem grammatica nil aliud est quam quaedam inalterabilis locutionis identitas diversis temporibus atque locis . . .* (I, 9).

Latin remained also, it goes without saying, the language of religious literature which continued to produce masterpieces. It is sufficient to mention the Office of the Holy Sacrament composed by St. Thomas Aquinas (1225-1274). The famous sequence *Lauda Sion Salvatorem* and the hymn *Pange Lingua Gloriosi* are still sung in our churches. Here again we should note that the exposition of doctrine was never sacrificed for lyricism. On the contrary, the latter was only raised so high because the dogmatic contents of each stanza, formulated with as much precision as an article of the *Summa,* furnished a solid base for the lyric transport of the next.

Saint Francis of Assisi (1182-1226) was at the source of a spring which refreshed and enlivened all spirituality. Emile Mâle has shown its influence upon the religious art of the end of the Middle Ages. It is no less strong in literature where it expresses itself in meditations upon the Passion. The cross which, in Fortunat's *Pange Lingua,* had been the glorious instrument of a sacrifice ending in triumph, is now the gibbet on which the Man of Sorrows died. It is upon this that St. Bonaventure (or the author of the *Laudismus de Santa Cruce*) invites us to meditate, while the Franciscan John

Pecham, later archbishop of Canterbury, composed his *Philomena*. The song of the nightingale which dies in the ecstasy of its passion typifies the cry of the soul aspiring to heaven.

The most poignant of these meditations at the foot of the cross is the *Stabat Mater,* too well known to need description. It is considered to be the work of Jacopone of Todi (1230-1306) who wrote *Laude* in Umbrian dialect—although only three later manuscripts ascribe it positively to him. At any rate, it is of Franciscan origin.

A Cistercian, Arnulf of Louvain (c. 1200-1250), monk, then abbot of Villers-en-Brabant, is the author of a long poem *De Passione Domini,* replete with ardent devotion to the wounds of Christ.

The *Dies Irae* of the Franciscan Thomas de Celano is (although similar verse occurred already in manuscripts of the 12th century) a good example of a kind which we have met in all its elements, but which now reached its highest perfection: the evocation of the grandiose scene represented so many times on the portals of the cathedrals . . . the expression of mingled fear and hope in souls at the thought of appearing before their Judge. The liturgy also welcomed very quickly what was simply a *pia meditatio.* The addition of the two last strophes made of it the sequence which we still hear in the Office of the Dead.

The Franciscan spirit also renewed hagiography. To tell the wonderful tale of the poor man of Assisi, Saint Bonaventure (d. 1274), the Seraphic Doctor who had reached the highest peaks of philosophic speculation in the Middle Ages, found words as simple and moving as those of the humble brother Leo whose *Speculum Perfectionis* (1227) was written on the very morrow of the death of Saint Francis.

Towards the middle of the century, the Dominican Jacobus de Voragine, bishop of Genoa (d. 1298), gave to hagiography its Summa: the *Golden Legend,* where he arranged, according to the liturgical year, the stories which he had read or heard told. His only purpose was to touch the heart. The success of his work made it a repertory from which artists were to draw the episodes which they translated into paintings.

Toward the end of the Middle Ages, the critical spirit was born. It manifested itself in a negative manner in parodies—parodies which show how conscious men had become of hagiographic technique. It was a game now to apply it to the composition of a *De Sancto Nemine* or a *De Sancto Invicem.* In a positive manner, criticism showed itself in an attentive vigilance which would stop short any popular embellishments which heresy is so prompt to seize upon. The Life of the Blessed Elizabeth of Erkenrode,[1] for example, is such an account as would be established today by a commission of priests or doctors to investigate a case of one marked with the stigmata.

Secular poetry was not extinct either. The poems of the 12th century were copied. The famous collection of the *Carmina Burana* (that is, of the abbey of Benedictbeuern) was made for a Bavarian patron toward the end of the 13th century; but its best pieces were much earlier. It is probable that the measures taken by the Church against the *clerici ribaldi* and the *vagi scholares* contributed to the drying up of a rich source of inspiration. It was not renewed, in any

[1] *Catalogus Codicum Hagiographicorum Bibl. Reg. Bruxell.* I, pp, 362-378.

case; and anonymity prevents us from distinguishing the new productions from those of the preceding century. A notable exception—which, however, concerns a didactic work—is the *Registrum Multorum Auctorum* (1280) by Hugo of Trimberg (ed. K. Langosch, 1942, *Germanische Studien* 235) which is the inventory in rhythmic verse of the *Antiqui* and *Moderni* read in the schools of his time. It is especially valuable to us because the works are identified by their *incipit*. Metric poetry offered nothing more remarkable unless perhaps it was the *Vado Mori* by the Dominican Lambert of Liége where the repetition of the sinister warning permitted eloquent amplifications which became monotonous at length. There are divers anonymous manuscripts of the 14th century. Poetry, too often, was the business of rhetoricians who had nothing to say. Even in the genres in which the Middle Ages showed itself most original (notably the animal fable) the prolixity of unskilful writers did it a disservice. The *Brunellus,* for example, written about 1200 in Southern Flanders,[2] takes 410 lines for a subject which Lafontaine (*Les Animaux Malades de la Peste*) treats in 64! And the narrative which demands humor and vivacity is cramped into monotonous distichs. Those who loved to read these fables preferred the time-worn prose (which at least went straight to the point) of the *Romulus* or the *Liber Parabolarum* of Odo of Cherinton.

In the same vein and in the same Latin, the *Gesta Romanorum* were compiled at the end of the 13th century for the edification and amusement of readers, but also to furnish the preachers with anecdotes suited to strike the imagination of the faithful. These were the *Exempla,* collections of which

[2] See Voigt, *Kleinere Lateinische Denkmaeler der Thiersage,* 1878.

began to multiply from the end of the 12th century. The most important ones are those which were translated into Latin from the French sermons of Jacques de Vitry (who was the biographer of Saint Marie de Oignies). Like those of analogous collections, they are bare of any literary ambition,[3] but they are full of details of customs, tales and fables of considerable interest to folklorists.

We must also mention here the *Dialogus Miraculorum* of the Cistercian Caesarius of Heisterbach (c. 1180-1245) in twelve books called *Distinctiones*. Their titles—on conversion, on temptation, on demons . . . —indicate quite clearly their edifying character. The Latin is simple and flowing and quite correct.

The vernacular comes through in the Latin of the *Chronicle* of Fra Salimbene de Adam (1221-c.1289), one of the most interesting of the Middle Ages. Its historical value would not make it worthy of mention if the Italian Franciscan did not appear in it as an extraordinarily engaging writer of memoirs of a picturesque freshness which we might be tempted to call Rabelaisian:—but Gilson shows us that, from the twelve years which he passed with the Grey Friars of Fontenay-le-Comte, Gargantua's father must have kept something "of the lively and homely spirit of the Franciscans."[4] Salimbene himself was an incarnation of the "average Franciscan . . . going from convent to convent and from province to province, collecting stories and telling them in such rich language that, reading it today, we can almost hear him speak" (p. 220).

[3] Cf. *Exempla aus Handschriften des Mittelalters*, ed. J. Klapper (Sammlung Mittellateinischer Texte, 1911, after the manuscripts of Breslau.)
[4] *Les Idées et les Lettres*, pp. 197 ff.

His geography of Franciscan France is very simple. It has eight provinces: four where one drinks wine, and four where one drinks beer. Here we recognize the bon vivant; but one must read his anecdotes (sometimes rather broad and often of a frank wantonness) to appreciate his talents as a writer.

In the 14th century, the *Philobiblon* of Richard Aungerville of Bury (1287-1345) is at the same time the work of a passionate bibliophile and of one of the savants "who best characterized the transition towards humanism," less by his style (which is a step backwards from the fine and calm elegance of John of Salisbury) than by his tendencies: "personal observation and individualism . . . a great and warm sympathy for the ideas of culture, knowledge and human progress." (Cf. the study of De Ghellinck, *Revue d'Histoire Ecclésiastique,* XVIII, 1922, pp. 271-312 and 482-508; XIX, 1923, pp. 157-200).

This is not the place to speak of Petrarch although he considered his *Africa,* a Latin epic, his bid for immortality. He was a man of the Renaissance.

Yet, at this very moment, a new wave of spiritual life appeared in the North. It found its expression in Flemish with Ruysbroek, in Latin with Gerard Groote (1340-1384) of Deventer. After having studied in Paris, Cologne and Prague, Groote retired to a Carthusian convent, and then began to preach against the corruption of the clergy with such a vehemence that he was silenced. From then on, grouping around him several disciples, he devoted himself to works of charity. This was the nucleus of the "Brethren of the Common Life"; but their first house was not founded until after Groote's death. It was, in 1387, the Congregation

of Windesheim whence the brotherhood of the same name
went out. The letters of instruction by Gerard Groote re-
mind us sometimes of St. Bernard; with the same vigilance
in respect to doctrine, the same pressing rebukes to bring
back to the fold the wandering sheep. This passionate vehemence explains the influence of a man whose spirituality,
turning from the mystic speculation of his master Ruysbroek, was practical.

It was at Deventer that Thomas Hammerken of Kempen
(a Kempis) (1380-1471) was educated. He entered the convent of Mt. St. Agnes near Zwolle and never left it. There
he wrote his treatises: *Soliloquium Animae, Vallis Liliarum,*
and most certainly also—although a number of other attributions have been proposed—the most famous book in all
Christianity after the Gospels: *The Imitation of Christ.* It is
so well known that we need not discuss it at length. It is
in the tradition reaching back to St. Bernard, which gave us
the resume of the doctrine in two words: *Ama nesciri.* It
represents, moreover, a return to the great masters of spirituality and through them, as the title indicates, a return to
the very source of all Christian religion. It was a reaction
against two centuries of scholastic subtleties and against the
aberrations of an epoch of feverish restlessness.[5] Thomas a
Kempis addressed himself to the Orders (cf. I, 19), but he
used a language so human and professed a doctrine so firm
that since then and without interruption, the book has had
the power to sustain Christians of all conditions, and that
even those who see in it only a purely human wisdom, find
in it the fruits of an experience which has penetrated beyond
our weakness and beyond the vanity of all the things of this

[5] See J. Huizinga, *The Waning of the Middle Ages,* 1924.

world. The language is as great as the doctrine: sober, a little too bare perhaps (it is not the open air of the Gospels where men were on a level with daily life; we are in a monk's cell) but the short sentences lift us to the highest summits. The rhyme which scans the cola, is never obtrusive; the sentiments are guarded; there is no pathos, nor bombast or affectation of any sort. In short, nothing in this firm and plain Latin could lead us to speak of decadence.

Erasmus also owed his early education to Deventer; but with the author of the *Adagia* and the *Colloquia* we definitely leave the Middle Ages.

The Middle Ages still lived on in schoolbooks such as the *Auctores Morales Octo,* a collection which grew little by little through the course of the centuries, and which exists in printed editions. There we find, among others, the moral precepts of the Pseudo-Cato, the *Ecloga Theoduli,* the *Facetus* (a handbook on how to live), the *Tobias* of Matthew of Vendôme, the *De Contemptu Mundi* of Bernard of Cluny, the *Parabolae* of Alan of Lille . . . Rabelais tells us how the young Gargantua wasted his time and effort with them before he came to Ponocrates. But these mediocre works have a tenacious life: we can follow the traces of the oldest of them, the Pseudo-Cato, for the longest time: up to Franklin and the wisdom of Poor Richard.

These are the last embers of the fire which was lighted by Boethius and Cassiodorus and which cast its last flame with the *Imitatio.* For ten centuries it had lighted the world and had assembled around its light the intelligences of all countries. The rise of national literatures, in spite of all their brilliance, will always leave with us the regret for a time when one universal language held together a community of thought and culture and perpetuated, among all the young nations who had been born of it, the unity of the old Empire of the West.

Select Bibliography

The following works are indispensable for a more detailed study of the subject than has been possible here:

Strecker, Karl, *Einfuehrung in das Mittellatein*. Third edition, Berlin 1939. French translation, revised and augmented by P. van den Woestijne: *Introduction à l'Etude du Latin Médiéval*. 3rd ed. Paris 1948. (*Société des Publications Romanes et Françaises*, XXVI).

De Ghellinck, J., S.J. *Littérature Latine au Moyen Age*. Paris 1939. (*Bibliothèque Catholique des Sciences Religieuses*). Two volumes have been published; this must be supplemented by: *L'Essor de la Littérature Latine au XIIᵉ Siècle, by the same author*. Brussels 1946.

For the last centuries of the Middle Ages, no comprehensive work exists; short notices on the most important writers may be found in:

Wright, F. A., and Sinclair, T. A., *A History of Later Latin Literature from the Middle of the Fourth to the End of the Seventeenth Century*. London 1931.

The most complete work for the history of the literature is the following:

Manitius, Max, *Geschichte der Lateinischen Literatur des Mittelalters*. (*Handbuch der Klassischen Altertumswissenschaft*, ed. Iwan Mueller). Three volumes. Munich 1911-1931.

After the 12th century, material may be found in:

Groeber, G., *Grundriss der Romanischen Philologie*, Vol. II, 1. Strasbourg 1893-1902.

For the history of poetry, the following are books worth reading. They also give a large number of quotations. Due to war-time difficulties in re-uniting texts and documentation, we have frequently taken recourse to them:

Raby, F. J. E., *A History of Christian Latin Poetry from the Beginning to the Close of the Middle Ages*. Oxford 1927.

Raby, F. J. E., *A History of Secular Latin Poetry in the Middle Ages*. Two volumes. Oxford 1934.

The texts are extremely scattered. The two most complete collections are the following:

Migne, *Patrologia Latina (P. L.)* Paris 1844 ff. (222 volumes, re-printing older editions some of which are now outdated).

Monumenta Germaniae Historica (M.G.H.), with their different sections: *Scriptores* (SS); *Auctores Antiquissimi; Scriptores Rerum Merowingicarum; Poetae Latini Aevi Carolini* (P. L.); *Scriptores Rerum Germanicarum in usum scholarum . . . separatim editi,* etc.
For the hagiographic texts:
   Acta Sanctorum. A Jo. Bollando et successoribus ab anno 1643 usque ad nostram aetatem diligenter edita *(AA. SS. Boll.)*
Numerous anthologies, among which we only mention the following:
   Beeson, Ch. H., *A Primer of Medieval Latin.* Chicago (*The Lake Classical Series*). It contains a useful introduction on the language and grammar of medieval texts.
   Harrington, K. P., *Medieval Latin, selected and edited.* Boston 1925. (*College Latin Series*).
For the lyrical poetry:
   The Oxford Book of Medieval Latin Verse. Ed. S. Gaselee, Oxford 1928 (reprinted 1946).
Numerous periodicals devote space to medieval Latin. Let us mention here:
   Speculum. A Journal of Medieval Studies (since 1926), the organ of the *Medieval Academy of America.*
   Archivum Latinitatis Medii Aevi (*A.L.M.A.*), or *Bulletin Du Cange* (since 1924), is devoted to questions of language and especially of lexicography: it is the organ of contact for the collaborators of the Dictionary which is being prepared under the auspices of the *Union Académique Internationale* and which is destined to replace the monumental *Glossarium Mediae et Infimae Latinitatis* (1678) of Du Cange and his continuators.

Index